Aspects
of
Loss

A Companion for Bereaved Parents and their Families

Gill Hartley

www.gillhartley.com

MOORLEYS
Print & Publishing

British Library Cataloguing in Publication Data.
A catalogue record for this book is available from the British Library

Front Cover and all illustrations by Diane Brazier
(Cover adapted from photo of Will)

ISBN 978 0 86071 655 6

MOORLEYS
Print & Publishing
23 Park Road, Ilkeston, Derbyshire DE7 5DA, England
0115 932 0643 - info@moorleys.co.uk - www.moorleys.co.uk

Contents

Dedication

For my precious son, Will

and

all grieving parents and their families

Acknowledgements

Chris Agee: I heard; It and In the End, from Next to Nothing, Salt Publishing; Kay Allen, from Edward's Trust, for her article in Fog and for her poem, Knots; Jean Beith for permission to quote from her poem, Silent Candle; Ian Campbell for his article, Blind Faith; Gina Claye, for Yesterday; Don't let them tell you how to grieve, The Photograph and Lighting a Candle, from Don't let them tell you how to grieve, OxPen; Visiting Hour by Stewart Conn from Stolen Light: Selected Poems (Bloodaxe Books, 199); Charles Coulson for Desktop Photos and The Unfinished Portrait; Jim Denning for The Cherry Tree from Pebbles, Debris and Other Poems; Julie Donnelly for The Look on Your Face Says it All; Kathy Duggan for Somersault; The Embrace from Sweet Machine by Mark Doty, published by Jonathan Cape. Reprinted by permission of the Random House Group Ltd; When I shall die, from Mister God, this is Anna. Reprinted by permission of Harper Collins Publishers Ltd © Fynn 1974 (year of original publication); Genesse Bourdeau Gentry for Why not ask me? Unspoken and Fences, from Stars in the Deepest Night, Writer's Club Press, 1999; Rev. Steve Griffiths for permission to quote from his book, God of the Valley; Michelle Gunner for Beyond Darkness; Mary Hartley for Names; Danielle Hope for her poems, Call, Contact, and Loss, from: City Fox, Rockingham Press; Rachel Irven for Something of the Child; Absence and Time Does Not Heal by Elizabeth Jennings: New Collected Poems, Carcanet; The C S Lewis Company Ltd for their kind permission to quote from his work; Edna St Vincent Millay Society: Time does not bring relief; Love has Gone, Sorrow, Dirge without Music and First Fig; Michael Mitton for Our God of Hope; Najwa Mounla for her article, Fog; Jan Moran Neil for White Rhino in Winter, from Serving Bluebird Pie and World Wide Writers Anthology and for Weep; Michael Rosen: One of us fell off the boat, from Carrying the Elephant; Laura Samson for When the grief takes hold; Carla Sheehan for the excerpt from A Nation Rocked to Sleep; Diane Shepherd for Cemetery, Reflexion, Wishing, Three Visits. Gone too Soon and End of Summer; Pat Sentinella for Only the silence of these empty rooms, Presentiment, Dried Grass in Winter; Muriel Stuart's daughter for her mother's poem, The Seed Shop; Tony Turner for Links from Reading the Signs and A Small Sherry Glass from Belief in Something Better; Jill Wallis for: Unforewarned and Last Night from Dialogue for One; Philip Wells: Walk out of the house of time, from Love is a Shining Language; Eileen Whatmough for When I first moved away and My Christmas has been Stolen; Sue White for: The Artist's Gift, Frozen in Time, Last Night, A Coat for all Seasons and for her prose.

Special thanks to Michael Rosen for kindly writing the foreword and for his poem. And to Joe Lawley, co-founder of TCF for permission to print his poem and quote his words.

I have genuinely sought to acknowledge all those whose quotations, poems and writings are used in this book, but if I have missed anyone I sincerely ask for their forbearance, and if they get in touch I will acknowledge them in any future reprint.

Gill Hartley.

Foreword
by
Michael Rosen

I don't think we know for certain why or how writing about loss and bereavement seems to help us but I'm going to have a go at it here. When we write, we do something slowly and deliberately, choosing words and phrases that matter. This seems to make us lay things out in an order. We give the mass of feelings whirling around in our heads some kind of shape. It's a way of sorting, and sorting figures largely in the way we humans survive and progress. People who can't and don't sort are people who find it quite difficult to cope with everyday things. So that part of writing which seems to be about sorting, is a way of helping us cope with these deeply sad things.

Then there's the matter of taking things out of yourself and putting them on a page in front of you. I think that this is a little bit like looking in a mirror or at a photo of yourself. Looking at what you've written is a way of appraising who you are and what you're about. You find yourself asking questions: am I really like that? Do I really think those things? Am I really that unhappy?

When you do this kind of evaluation of yourself, I think it gives you a springboard from which you can plan to do new things. You can't and don't stay in exactly the same place. But then something else comes into play - and this is why Gill Hartley's book is so important - you start to share what you've written. And there are at least two ways of sharing going on here: there's the sharing with people who've had similar experiences, and this enables us to wonder if we are like or unlike other people. And there is the sharing with people who have little or no idea what it feels like. And that can take you into new territory too. You see in people's faces and in the words they say, the anguish and sympathy they have for your situation. And that is helpful too. It's yet another way to rediscover that you are part of the human race and we all need each other.

After all, there are times when those of us who've had this particular part of bereavement feel that we aren't really part of this world - and in the end we all lose someone; we are all left by someone at some time. We thought for a moment that it was only us who had this happen to them; it was only me who felt this bad. True, but not true!

So I wish this book and all who sail in her, the best of lives. Or, as people say in the Jewish tradition, 'Long life!'

Michael Rosen

The silence after lasts forever
It is as quiet in the second it ended
as it is years later.
Quieter than a painting.
There is nothing as quiet as this.
It is as quiet as nothing.
Michael Rosen

Introduction...

The moment you died
I felt an instant of joy.
No more suffering
for you, but my darling son
mine had only just begun...

Gill Hartley

Our dearly loved son, Will, died in January 2006 at the age of twenty-two. It still seems impossible. Where have I been in the years since he died and what have I done with them?

What have I done? Well, I have written a book of poems dedicated to Will, which was published in 2008 and the book you are reading now. I at last found the courage to put together a collage of photographs of Will: from his first photo with me holding him, shortly after he was born, right up to the most recent. When I was putting the collage together, it struck me how we take so many photographs of our children when they are small but less as they grow into adulthood. Will had become a keen photographer, so not only do we have boxes of photos we took, but his to treasure too. And can we part with any of them? No. Not even the duplicates.

What else have I done? I have made some wonderful friends, learned to let old friendships go – create a new address book, so to speak. I have learned new computer skills, no longer being able to rely on Will for help. And I can now send text messages. Why couldn't I do that before? Because Will had set my mobile onto pre-emptive text and I couldn't handle that. And I have learned to act, to wear the mask we all learn to wear to keep others happy.

But where have I been during those years? Struggling. Defending myself. Making excuses. Trying to prove that I can cope. It is only now, now that I am having counselling, that I am beginning to realise that one thing I have not really allowed myself to do is grieve. Really, truly, grieve.

Yes, of course I **have** grieved. I ploughed through the wilderness of the first year, numb and senseless – really believing I was losing my mind. I trawled through book after book related to loss, suffering, the death of a child or children, the afterlife. I spent hours endlessly reliving what had happened to Will, desperately trying to rewrite it all; to make everything all right again; to bring him back. I wept, howled and screamed. Sometimes I sat, rocking to and fro, hugging a pillow wrapped in one of Will's tee shirts. At other times I just pleaded with God to let me die. I used to plead this for my husband, Edwin, (Will's father) as well but he wasn't so pleased when I told him! Unlike me, he never felt he wanted to die.

So why do I feel I have not truly grieved? Because I was obsessed with keeping up appearances, keeping up the traditional British stiff upper lip. Above all, I could not bear others to think me weak. Some of this was a result of a difficult childhood but much of it was to do with pride. Pride; one of the seven deadly sins. This was triggered by the realisation that I was on my own – that friends and family could not understand the depth of my pain. Only one friend offered to come and cry with me and, oddly enough, although I did see her, we never did weep together. Pride, yet again. The year after Will died, we visited a couple who had just lost their young son and, like us, their only child. When we met them, they both wept. Wept over Will's photo. Wept as they told their story. On the way home, I commented to Edwin that there was a sense in which I envied them for their ability to show their grief so openly. Why couldn't I have allowed myself to do that? Some reading this might say, well tears are private and I understand and respect that view. I stopped attending church, because I felt uncomfortable weeping every week in front of everyone. In many ways, our tears are private and our grief intensely personal.

But what I realise now, is that by not letting others see the true depth of my pain and agony, I have done myself and other bereaved parents a disservice.

Heaven knows we need never be ashamed of our tears, for they are rain upon the blinding dust of earth, overlying our hard hearts.
Charles Dickens

Unless we allow others to see our raw pain, let them see that we are devastated, ripped apart, broken by our loss, how can we expect them to begin to understand? It is human nature for others to want to make us feel better, to stick a plaster on our wound and say, "There, there…" But by putting on our masks, we are missing out. I did not understand that at the time. Perhaps it would not have made any difference if I had wept, said it how it was. But it might have done.

Maybe I am being too hard on myself and others. I think in the very, very early days, when we returned shell-shocked and numbed to our village, I did try to express my grief. But the support I so longed for and needed was simply not there. People did not know what to say and mostly stayed away.

After creating the collage of photographs of Will, I wished I had found the courage to do it before, because now if anyone comes to see us they cannot avoid looking at the photographs. It gives us a precious opportunity to talk about Will, to discuss the various occasions on which the photographs were taken. It provides us with a brief but valuable opportunity to talk about him. And something else looking at the photographs locks into is the time we have now spent without Will. During the first few years of his life, he grew from a gorgeous baby into a schoolboy, with all the accompanying and delightful stages of his infancy. It makes the years we have spent without him even more symbolic and I wonder what changes we would have seen in him over these now missing years and what he would be doing now.

I realise now that we cannot submerge our grief, bury it under a false pretension that we are coping. We cannot allow pride to let us do that. I have read in the past about delayed grief; that it will catch up with us sooner or later. And the more we smother it in activity and bravery, the more harm we do to ourselves. By saying this, I do not mean that we should not seek ways to honour our child, given our circumstances; the majority of us do. But we must be aware that we have suffered one of the deepest wounds a human soul can endure. We must allow our grief to surface, if we lock it away under a mantle of busyness, we do so at our peril – we run the risk of ill health, depression and spiritual loneliness.

To those parents reading this who have just embarked on this lonely and desperate road, please know you are not alone. There are many of us who have suffered like you. But please let us be honest with our grief. Let us not hide our feelings; let others see our tears. Some, like me, may find it difficult to do that but surely we owe it to our dear children to smother our pride and let rip with our grief. They are worth it. Every single tear…

River
Standing alone
But together, hand in hand
Washed by torrential tears
Cleansing

Edwin Hartley

In the numbing weeks and months after Will died, I read book after book on grief, bereavement, the afterlife, theology and anthologies of poetry and prose, in a desperate quest to make some sense of it all. I would dip in into these books, reaching out for one every time I woke in the night. I know many parents react this way and, like me, read endlessly. The idea for this book came from that early experience and I hope will help to fulfil the need we have for a book we can pick up at any time and dip into.

Elizabeth Kubler Ross was the first person to put grief into stages – she later regretted this – but people took it as a blueprint and, sadly, it is used by many today to judge our reaction to bereavement and how we deal with it. Whilst I recognise the titles she has given these so-called stages, I do not believe that they come in sequence and, especially when the loss is as catastrophic as the loss of a child, the pattern is fragmented. For this reason, I have divided this book into sections but given each one a heading which I believe more aptly describes the different turnings our never-ending journey takes us on.

"Stages of grief - shock, denial, numbness, guilt, rage, misery and resolution? Rubbish"

Virginia Ironside
"You'll get over it – the rage of bereavement"

I think the following words from Robert Veninga captures beautifully the way our grief has no set pattern.

Human pain does not let go of its grip at one point in time. Rather it works its way out of our consciousness over time. There is a season of sadness. A season of anger. A season of hope. A season of tranquillity. But seasons do not follow one another in lockstep manner. At least not for those in crisis. The winters and springs of one's life are all jumbled together in a puzzling array. One day we feel as if the dark clouds have lifted, but the next day they have returned. One moment we can smile but a few hours later the tears emerge... It is true that as we take two steps forward in our journey, we may take one or two steps backward. But when one affirms that the spring will arrive, the winter winds seem to lose some of their punch.

Robert Veninga
A Gift of Hope: How we survive our tragedies.

I have included some of the articles I wrote for the Compassionate Friends quarterly journal, as I struggled along this tortuous road. You may not agree with all I have written but I hope you will identify with some of my thoughts. Looking back now, I think one thing that these articles do reflect is just how many times we take a step forward, only to take several steps back soon after.

We all have a unique and special relationship with our children and when we lose them, our world changes forever. Nothing will ever be the same again. But no matter how short our child's life, one thing is certain. The time we spent with them in our lives was precious and we hope that, in time, we will look back at those years with joy, albeit our joy is mingled with our tears...

There is sacredness in tears. They are not the mark of weakness, but of power. They speak more eloquently than ten thousand tongues. They are the messengers of overwhelming grief, of deep contrition, and of unspeakable love.

Washington Irving

Will aged twenty-one. 12th May 2005

I took this photo of Will when we travelled on the Orient Express to Stratford upon Avon to celebrate my sixtieth birthday. I had always longed to travel on this legendary train and when we found that we could take a day trip, it was a dream realised.

This is the stuff
of which dreams are made,
am I really here with you?
Your eyes, are they truly smiling
at me?
And your touch, so soft,
is it true?

This is the stuff
of which dreams are made,
I can feel your breath on my
cheek,
Hear your voice,
saying, "I love you, Mum."
is this real...
or a dream that I seek?

Will's story...

Will's death came as a shock to all who knew and loved him. Until he first became unwell in September the previous year, he had been fit and healthy. He was just over six feet in height, and with his amazing silvery blond hair, hazel eyes and golden skin, he was a beautiful young man. His quiet unassuming manner belied a wacky, but dry, sense of humour and he had the ability to relate to everyone he met, whatever their age.

Will was bright at school. He was popular with his teachers, who loved him for his enthusiasm and friendliness, as well as his aptitude for learning. I treasure the comment made by the teacher in his reception class who, when I collected Will after his first day at school, commented, "I am very pleased with him," and later added, "There's the rest of the class - and there's William."

All parents think their children are special, and of course they are. Every child is precious and unique. Will had that quality that made people single him out. When I took him in his pushchair to the weekly market, the stallholders would always stop me to talk to him, or have some treat for him. I used to worry that he was too friendly, too outgoing, but, as he grew older, he became shyer.

I never wanted Will to be an only child. I grew up next door to a couple that had lost their only child, Jack, in a cycling accident when he was sixteen. His death destroyed their happiness. They doted on my brother, sister and me, but seeing the havoc Jack's death wreaked in their lives, I vowed even then that I would never have an only child.

But life doesn't always deal its cards the way we want and after Will was born, by emergency caesarean, I was never able to conceive again. I tried to compensate by inviting his friends to play, as there were no children of his age within my own family. Fortunately, he always had the ability to enjoy his own company and would chatter non-stop to himself, as he created imaginary scenarios with his adored Lego.

I loved every minute of his childhood. He was a delight to be with and so interested in everything. He would happily accompany me to garden nurseries, to Kew Gardens, the kind of places many children of his age found boring. I worked at a local residential centre for adults with cerebral palsy, where I taught art. Will often came with us on our annual day out, usually to an art gallery or museum. He was never daunted by physical disability and was very popular with the residents. Will and I were always close and that closeness grew as the years passed.

When Will was seventeen and at Grammar School, I attended an Alpha course at our local church and became a Christian. Although from childhood I had attended church and been confirmed, I did not really understand the Gospel message until I took the Alpha course. When I attempted to tell Will about my belief, he resisted initially, saying that he did not know what he thought. However a friend cleverly suggested he might like to attend a discussion with four or five young people around his age, at the church, as they would welcome someone with an opposing viewpoint.

To my surprise, Will agreed, but then he never could resist a good debate! Not long after this he went with the group to a Christian youth meeting. I was in bed reading when I heard him arrive home. He came running upstairs and, kneeling beside my bed and with tears streaming down his face, told me of his encounter with Christ. Others had been praying for him, he said, when his knees began to tremble, his eyelids to flicker, and he felt a hand grasp one of his outstretched hands. Then he described how he was running, impossibly fast, alongside a figure dressed in white, whom he could not see but knew to be Jesus. Together they raced up over impossibly steep hills and mountains, amongst the most incredible scenery. When it stopped, Will said he wept tears of remorse, saying over and over again, "I am so sorry I never noticed You before, I am so sorry."

Only when you drink from the river of silence shall you indeed sing.
And when you have reached the mountain top, then you shall begin to climb.
And when the earth shall claim your limbs, then you shall truly dance.

Kahlil Gibran from The Prophet

Will's description of his experience, coming from my sensible, level-headed teenager, convinced me that his experience was real, not imagined. From that moment on he became a committed Christian, uncompromising in his faith. He was confirmed when he was eighteen.

2

In a sense, I was not totally surprised by Will's conversion experience. When he was a small child and I took him to church, his eyes would always fill with tears when a Taizé refrain was sung. I was always aware of the spiritual side of Will.

Will gained a place at Birmingham University, to read History. Birmingham was his first choice and he was very happy there. Knowing he was a Christian gave me much peace of mind, knowing what students can get up to in their first year at university! I needn't have worried. I always felt God looked after Will during his time at Birmingham. The first year, when he was in one of the halls of residence, there were other Christians on his corridor and some Christian girls in the adjoining corridor. Like all new students, Will made the most of his first year at university, doing the usual rounds of clubs and pubs, enjoying the freedom that all students relish in their first year. But the friends he made were all like Will; honest, genuine young people. When he subsequently moved on to share a house with four of those lads from his corridor, they never embarrassed Will by bringing girls home for the night. And one of the four was also, like Will, a Christian.

The subject Will chose for his dissertation was Byzantium Iconoclasm. He chose this subject because it combined his love of history with his interest in Theology and he was also fascinated by Byzantium. I can't tell you how many times I have tried, as a layman, to explain to people what that entailed. He worked hard and, to our delight, gained a first degree honours.

As close as we were, it was still difficult for Will to come back home to live, having spent three years away and tasted what it was like to be independent. Until he found employment, he would not be able to afford to rent his own place, or even to share with others. However, finding employment proved harder than he expected. Especially so, because Will found that much as he searched the vacancy advertisements, he could not decide what career he wanted to pursue. To pass the time he took temporary employment and the following summer accompanied me to New Wine, an annual Christian camp, in Somerset. By the end of the week, Will knew where his future lay. He wanted to enter the Anglican Church. He wanted to train as a vicar. He was so excited. I remember him saying that once he felt God's call, there was nothing else he would rather do.

We were thrilled at Will's decision. He knew that by becoming a vicar he would never earn a lot of money but that was unimportant to him. He had begun to re-evaluate his life and its purpose. He knew he had not chosen an easy career but was sure it was right for him. I think he was a little surprised by the initial response to his application. We all thought that the church would be delighted to have someone his age enter the ministry. We had often heard the Anglican Church called the "Greying Church" due to the number of people undertaking ministry work who were close to retirement age. His first interview was not encouraging. He was told he was too young and to go away and gain more life experience. But he persisted and his second interview was successful. Will worked hard, with the support of our vicar, to gain as much experience as possible in order to give him the best chance of being accepted for training as a minister. He joined the PCC, became a Deanery Synod representative for our church and, at the age of twenty-two, became leader of a newly formed cell group. One of the comments made at Will's service was that it said a lot about Will that he was in charge of a group whose ages spanned fifty years.

In October 2005, Will travelled to Edinburgh for a friend's birthday. He arrived home full of enthusiasm for the city of Edinburgh and its yearly festival and eager to show us the photographs and slides he had taken. It was shortly after this trip that Will first began to feel unwell; he seemed extremely tired and complained of a strange sensation in his legs.

We took Will to see a neurologist, who immediately diagnosed Multiple Sclerosis.

I can't tell you how many times we have regretted not seeking a second opinion, as after Will died there were some doubts as to whether the diagnosis of MS was correct in the first place. This obviously had come as a devastating blow to Will and to us. He feared it would stop him pursuing the career in the church. Although we have found out since that there was no reason that the diagnosis should stand his way, sadly this was not the impression that Will was given by the church at the time. Will had an MRI scan, which appeared to confirm the diagnosis of MS and he became increasingly depressed and dispirited. In November 2005, I took him to Norfolk, in the hopes that a break from everything might lift his spirits. It was a difficult week; Will was very tired but kept putting the fatigue and other odd symptoms he was experiencing, down to the MS. Despite all this, we both loved the Norfolk coast and made plans to return there for Will's birthday in March, this time with his father as well. I could never have imagined this would not happen and we would never go away together again.

After we arrived home, Will went to see a GP at our local practice, who diagnosed depression. But I became increasingly worried and two days later we went back to the doctor's, this time to see our own GP. She was immediately concerned and sent us to the local hospital for a second opinion on what appeared to be a chest infection. It still haunts me that when I drove Will to see our GP that morning, he would never again return home. Within two hours, he was in intensive care.

Will was at our local hospital for the first three days, before being transferred to a hospital in Leicester, where he was put on to an ECMO, a kind of modern lung by-pass, for five days. Initially he seemed to improve after coming off the ECMO but it was not to be.

I cannot write about the ensuing weeks, it is too painful and distressing. We hoped and prayed (along with literally hundreds of people) that he would recover but the doctors never knew what they were treating and, after six traumatic weeks, we lost him. We were with him when he died. The post mortem showed no evidence of MS but a cause for Will's illness was never established. It was a cruel six weeks, for much of the time Will was rendered unconscious and on the precious occasions he was conscious he was unable to talk with us because he had a tracheotomy. He could only write on a pad, held by the nurse or by us.

Throughout it all, he remained gracious and kind, concerned for the nurses and those who had travelled from our village to visit him. I always cherish the memory of his kindness to the cleaner, who regularly cleaned his room. She often talked of her two sons, obviously thrilled that they had both gone to university. One day when she came into Will's room, he held out his hand to her. Delighted, she hurried to remove her gloves and wash her hands. Then she stood, by Will's bed, holding his hand and he hung on every word as she told him all about her sons. His eyes never left her face. I am sure she will never forget that moment. I know I won't – I was so proud to be his mother.

Everyone was devastated when Will died. The doctors and nurses wept. His funeral was incredible; our church was absolutely packed, with people in the entrance lobby and the hall as well. We raised the roof for one and a half hours with Will's favourite worship songs and listened to the wonderful tributes to our very special son.

I'm looking at this photograph of me,
taken on my birthday
the year before you went away.
We travelled on the Orient Express,
something I'd always longed to do.
I bought you a suit, a pink shirt,
and new tie. You looked very handsome
and I was so proud of you.
The sun shone and it was a perfect time,
a day I will remember until I die.
But none of this explains my smile
in this photo that you took,
a special smile I no longer have,
the radiance, the sparkle in my eyes,
was there, my son, because I smiled at...
you.

I found the following words in one of the many books I devoured after Will died. They were from an old headstone and I thought them very poignant.

If only we could SEE the splendour of the land,
To which our loved ones are called from you and me,
We'd understand.

If only we could HEAR the welcome they receive,
From the old familiar voices all so clear,
We would not grieve.

If only we could KNOW the reason why they went,
We'd smile and wipe away the tears that flow,
And wait content.

Anon

A tomb is not a blind alley, it is a
thoroughfare. It closes in the twilight and
opens on the dawn.

Anon

Will is buried at Little Marlow cemetery. A member of "Memorials by Artists", who lives near High Wycombe, created a stunningly simple headstone for Will out of Welsh slate. On the front he has carved the words:

Will

1983 – 2006

Fog

In the days and weeks following the death of a beloved child, we are thrust into a foreign country and nothing makes sense any more. I have called this section, "Fog" because it is exactly how it feels – we are lost. Even faces and places we know well seem unfamiliar to us. Some of the things that happened or that were said to us during those early days stand out in my memory, like the signs we see when we are driving in fog. But much of it is blurred and confused. Many people having endured the agony of watching a loved one die, describe walking out of the hospital or their home and being faced with a world that has suddenly become totally unfamiliar and somehow too bright. It sounds a contradiction to say that when I am using the analogy of fog but in many ways it is similar, due to the feeling of disorientation we experience.

Najwa Mounla wrote the following article for the TCF journal "Compassion".

As a bereaved parent I often heard this phrase "I am in the fog" but have not quite understood it until I was actually driving in thick fog.

It was 14 months after Haas, our only son, died. We found it difficult to spend Christmas holidays at home. We decided to go away to France, Val De Loire, a quiet area we know and like. We crossed the channel by ferry and drove our car to a Hotel where we had booked for one night in a village 20 miles off the motorway.

But this was December 08 and the worst winter France has known in 25 years. Peter, an experienced driver, was behind the wheel. Snow, frost and sleet were everywhere. Suddenly, we hit thick fog. Peter had to focus really hard to stay within the limits of the road. I had to gaze intensely to read the directions that lead us safely to our Hotel.

Peter held the steering tight. In front of him he could see a space of few meters only, enough to keep the car moving. I saw only whiteness. Fog was everywhere, a thick wall surrounding us. There was only one way to go and that was to drive ahead through the thick fog. We became stressed out and exhausted.

I was frightened we could skid. In fact, I was trembling with fear. I clenched my teeth. My throat was dry. Then, my memory failed me. I forgot the name of the village and the address of the Hotel where we were heading. Peter and I started arguing.

Along the way, we found ourselves comforted every time we passed through a thinner patch of fog. We relaxed whenever we saw the light of other cars crossing our way. We thought if other cars can drive safely in the fog, then we can do so as well.

Now I understand how a bereaved parent is living in the fog. Surely, we have poor visibility. There is no way to go except to move on through the fog. Death is an event that is forced upon us. We can do nothing to bring back our son. We have to accept our fate and go through the fog. We know we may develop ailing physical symptoms such as forgetfulness, headaches and constant fatigue. We know we may be angry sometimes and start arguing with our surviving loved ones. As bereaved parents, we survive the day by living one step at a time.

While driving in thick fog we were comforted to see other cars drive by. So it is in our bereavement, we are comforted by meeting compassionate friends who have experienced a similar loss. This brings us courage and hope. And as the fog clears in patches so does our grief. We are starting to see patches of hope in our daily life and we are gradually learning to cope with our loss.

My cousin, who is a vicar in Nottingham, was very supportive throughout the time Will was in hospital in Leicester. When Will died he came to pray with us and took us back to his home to stay for a few days with him and his family. He helped Edwin with the necessary formalities that had to be seen to, such as registering Will's death and contacting the undertakers near our home.

I could not do anything. I could not think clearly. All I did know was that I wanted to die and be with Will.

> *Leaves are falling; it's the end of summer,*
> *and the end of summer in my life,*
> *now I can only dwell in darkness,*
> *for when you left my day became my night.*

Now I have no need of sunshine,
nor moonlight nor the glow of stars,
I only want the gentle sound of silence,
I want no music or the song of birds.
There is no sign of any landscape,
the road ahead is flat and bleak,
I see no trees or flowers by the roadside,
no nestling hills or flowing streams.

Now you have gone my life is over,
I am now an empty shell.
Although my heart still beats it's broken,
I live on beneath this winter pall.   **Gill Hartley**

It is now over five years since the death of my son as I am compiling this book. To those who have not experienced a loss of this magnitude, five years may seem a long time. But to those "in the know" we remain in the early days of our grief. I still struggle to believe Will has gone and that I will not see him again in this life. Even now it seems impossible. I can still drive home sometimes, fantasising that I will find Will sitting in the living room and imagine him saying, "Where have you been, Mum? I've been looking for you."

Many parents have talked about the sense of unreality that stays with them for some years after the death of their child. We find ourselves wondering if our child was ever here? Did we dream it all? We know it is not a dream but at such times it helps to hold something that belonged to our child, something that provides tangible evidence of the wonderful times we spent with them.

When we were staying with my cousin in Nottingham the first few days after Will died, I went upstairs to get something out of my suitcase and in the case found a tee shirt belonging to Will. I can still remember hearing an unearthly primitive cry and realising that it was me – the sound was like nothing I had ever heard before and seemed to come from the very depths of my being. My cousin's wife came running up the stairs to hold me and, in her arms, I wept…

Casey Sheehan died in Iraq and his sister, Carly, wrote a poem which has captured the emotion and anger felt by so many bereaved parents at the seeming waste of so many young lives. The following stanza is from

11

this poem, **A Nation Rocked to Sleep,** which Carly has kindly given me permission to include in this anthology.

Have you ever heard the sound of a mother screaming for her son?
The torrential storms of weeping will never be done.
They call him a hero of that you should be glad.
But have you ever heard the sound of a mother screaming for her son?

The following poems capture the feelings of unreality and the extra-ordinary feelings some parents experience when they wonder not only who they themselves are but whether indeed their child actually existed.

Reality Check
Do I really know who I am?
I've lost myself since you died,
But, maybe it was always like this,
no identity I can recognise.
It seems I am standing alongside myself,
observing my every move,
the tears I shed are crocodile tears,
even when shed for you.
I know the pain is real enough,
my grief is absolute,
but the tears when they fall
seem so unreal,
for none of this can be true.

Did you really exist, my love,
were you truly my son?
Perhaps you were an Angel -
God-sent, on loan, to me.
If you were, my role as your mother
was not meant to be long.
Perhaps with God's grace
I will find a new song
now that you have gone...

Gill Hartley

I cannot say and I will not say
That he is dead. He is just away.
With a cheery smile, and a wave of the hand,
he has wandered into an unknown land
and left us dreaming how very fair
it needs must be, since he lingers there.

And you...oh you, who the wildest yearn
for an old-time step, and the glad return,
Think of him faring on, as dear
in the love of there as here.
Think of him still as the same, I say,
He is not dead - he is just away.

James Whitcomb Riley

Sad Song

You're away again
And absence is everywhere:
   In the stillness of your room
   The guitar uncased lies where you laid it
   And those last blue notes
   Have diminished too.
Absence is everywhere
And you're away again.

You're no longer here
And absence is the only refrain:
   In derelict fairground,
   On winter promenade,
   Storm-broken pier, unwalked-on sands,
   In dripping waters from tide-left wrecks
Absence is the only refrain
And you're no longer here.

Will you ever be here again
And absence never here again?
   Fresh hawthorn green has broken through,
   Our southerly wind is blowing warm,
   The dog-rose buds are filling
   And there's promise in each dawn:
Will absence never be here again?   **Barrie Shaw**

When Will died, I was, for some time, on another planet. I said things I would never think to say now, such as saying that I understood why God had "allowed" Will to die. I sincerely believed that the world was going to come to an end very shortly and that was why Will's ministry was so brief. I believed that the impact of his death and the strength of his faith amidst his dreadful suffering would bring others to find God before it was too late. I don't believe that now, of course. But, in the strange world I was occupying at the time, it felt logical. When the world did not come to an immediate end, I experienced an overwhelming need to keep talking about what had happened to Will. I think I believed that if enough people agreed how wrong it was, God would realise he had made a mistake and send Will back. After recognising this, I was intrigued to read in a book by Elizabeth Kubler Ross, that this is a common belief in those grieving deeply and something that she would describe as a part of the bargaining "process".

What I also found, to my surprise and great sadness, was that others could not understand the depth of my pain. I cover some of these feelings later on in this book but it came as a shock when I first experienced this lack of understanding. Because most of the people I knew had not lost a child, they could only relate my loss to their own experience of bereavement and, using this as a guide, began to utter the clichés I soon became all too familiar with.

Why, when faced with our grief,
Do some feel the need to say:
"Time heals all wounds."
"You will move on."
"Are you getting over it now?"

Why can't they simply,
Admit they are lost for words.
Why, in this culture of ours,
Are we so bad at dealing with grief?
Why can't we honest,
And speak the brutal truth,
That life is cruel and you are dead,
And we will always miss you.

Gill Hartley

Oppress'd with grief, oppress'd with care,
A burden more than I can bear,
Robert Burns

Four months after Will's death, I went on a few days retreat to an Anglican convent in Wantage, near Oxford. The elderly nun, with whom I was assigned to talk, was wonderfully understanding and compassionate. Although she had never married and had children, she showed more empathy than many people I encountered at that time. I came away feeling I had been given permission to grieve and that it was acceptable to fall apart and be angry with God.

Whilst at the convent, I raided the small library; in one of the books I found the following extract from a poem and copied it out into the journal I was keeping for Will. I have been unable to trace the full poem, or learn more about the writer, despite searching on the Internet. But it made me weep and locked into my pain.

Who will comfort a mother who has lost her son?
Who will give her refuge?
Who will shelter her in the dark night of grief?
To whom can she turn?
*   -   the linnet, terrified by the shouting, flies away...*
*   -   the lips of the beloved disciple are sealed by grief.*
Who will console her?
She is alone, the Mother of God.
She is forsaken – trodden down like grass –
She falls to the ground
(motionless like a corpse) but again she rose up.
A groaning pierced her heart through and through.
Her hair was in disarray:
(her head was spinning) her sight was blurred;
She ran headlong down the street
*   and she saw the Son.*
A heavy cross weighed down His shoulders.
His knees sagged under the blows:
and at every step He bent nearer and nearer
*   to the ground.*
With her head unveiled, overcome by woe
and stumbling,
the Mother of God followed behind Christ.
Aleksej Remizov from Theotokos 1989

Crucifixion

Mary Magdalene smote her breast and wept,
the disciple whom He loved turned to stone,
but where the Mother stood in silence
nobody even dared to look.

Anna Akkmatova
From Requiem 135 –1940

The following poems reflect my pain and longing during those very early days when I wanted nothing but to die and be with my son.

I'm weary now, and feel so very tired,
tired of living life without you here.
So tired of having to pretend
my life is back to normal when it's not.
I no longer have the energy to try
and keep pretending that I am all right,
whilst living with the knowledge you have gone.
My darling, I am so very tired,
I cannot find the strength to carry on
and live this life that's empty without you.
But I know I do not have a choice
my life is not in my hands but in God's..

Gill Hartley

I'm sorry but...

I'm sorry but I don't feel brave,
I don't think I can face the world.
I don't know how to find the strength,
I don't want to go on anymore.

The pain I carry inside me,
grows with each passing day,
time isn't making it better,
it just goes on getting worse.

I'm finding life unbearable,
I don't think I can live without you,
I sometimes can't make the effort,
to do anything at all.

16

It would be so much easier,
if God would just let me die,
then I could join you, my darling,
get away from this pain filled life.

But I know it isn't that simple,
I must live my allotted time,
but my life as I knew it is over,
from now I can only survive.

Gill Hartley

You are not here. I know that you are gone,
And will not ever enter here again.
And yet it seems to me, if I should speak,
Your silent step must wake across the hall;
If I should turn my head, that your sweet eyes
Would kiss me from the door. – So short a time
To teach my life its transposition to
This difficult and unaccustomed key! –
The room is as you left it; your last touch –
A thoughtless pressure, knowing not itself
As saintly – hallows now each simple thing;
Hallows and glorifies, and glows between
The dust's grey fingers like a shielded light.

There is your book, just as you laid it down,
Face to the table, – I cannot believe
That you are gone! – Just then it seemed to me
You must be here. I almost laughed to think
How like reality the dream had been;
Yet knew before I laughed, and so was still.
That book, outspread, just as you laid it down!
Perhaps you thought, "I wonder what comes next,
And whether this or this will be the end";
So rose, and left it, thinking to return.

Edna St Vincent Millay

17

Reflection

It comes naturally to some, the written word
of love and loss. Mine? Trite, absurd.
But I keep trying

To create something lovely, worthwhile,
to remember
to bring kind April into cold December.
How to do this? Mystifying.

Death of a child. Marks on a page.
Inspiration fails me. My age?
Not lovely or worthwhile, your dying

Diane Shepherd

When we first lost Will and I heard people say that a time would come when I did not think about Will all the time, I felt angry. Now I understand what they meant but it is not because I do not think about him. I do - every minute of every day but in a different kind of way from before. I am always conscious of his absence in my life and he is a part of everything I do and say. What has changed is that I do not sit and think only of him and nothing else. As time passes, I think we somehow internalise our love and grief - our lost child becomes part of the person we have become since their death. He is now part of me and always will be. The following poem was written in the early days of my grief, when thoughts of Will were all consuming.

Keep turning...Keeping turning...Keep turning...

You are always before me,
I am always thinking of you,
Like a watermill,
That keeps turning
You are constantly on my mind.

No matter what I am doing
Or with whom I am talking,
Whatever distraction I immerse myself in
I am always thinking of you.
Like a watermill
That keeps turning,
You are constantly on my mind.

And yet I never dream of you
Although I so, so wish I could,
In those sleeping moments
It's as if you are stolen from me
Strange, when every waking moment
I am always thinking of you.
Like a watermill
That keeps turning
You are constantly on my mind.

With God's grace, I know
A time will come
When I don't think constantly of you
For then we will be together,
Together, for the rest of time.
But until then,
My precious son,
I will always be thinking of you.
Like a watermill
That keeps turning
You will be constantly on my mind.
                                                    Gill Hartley

Kay Allen, who works for the Edward's Trust in Birmingham, describes so well the unreality and numbness of the early days following such a loss...

Just before Easter in March 1997 our youngest daughter Flora died. She had been born with a metabolic disease which was known to be life limiting, but her death came with little warning, while we were all asleep.

There is no precedent to prepare you for the death of your child. It is totally uncharted territory, there is no map and you don't have a compass. If you are blessed you may however find a guide, generally someone who has been there before you. But much of the journey will be spent alone, for grief is as individual as the person experiencing it.

The first days and weeks can only be described as totally surreal. Shocked and numb, you go about your daily business;

19

you find yourself standing in a shop with no idea how you got there or what you came in for. Some people have described the feeling as being underwater; for me it felt like wading through treacle, feeling pulled down while life carried on around me. I hoped to wake up to find it had all been a nightmare and not real at all.

At the same time I felt 'on alert' for some indication that Flora was coming back – a perpetual sensation of waiting for some message or sign, for which everything else must be put on hold. I constantly felt that there was something I should be doing but I knew not what. I now know that this period of grief is known as 'searching' for the person who is gone. When someone has been in your life and then is suddenly no longer present, it is only natural that you feel that they are around somewhere and expect their imminent return. This feeling is very distressing and can go on for a very long time, until emotionally you realise that they are not coming back. It is not enough to know it logically, in your head.

Loss this overwhelming is often described as emptiness, and indeed there was often a feeling of 'empty arms' that is described by bereaved parents. I felt insubstantial, a feeling that if I passed my hand over the centre of my body there would be nothing but a gaping hole. This emptiness extended to the world around me. Sitting in the house one day, I had the sudden sensation that the centre of the room was caving in.

I felt that the world had literally been turned upside down, so much so that I could not trust the ground to remain beneath my feet as I walked along and would feel that at any moment I might pitch headlong through the pavement.

These physical sensations were as nothing compared to the mental torment of my grief. I am a firm believer that we each have a pattern of how we deal with the things that happen to us, and my way of dealing with events is to obsess over them until I have fully thought them through. Thus I entered into a period of constant obsessive thinking which in grief work is known as 'rumination'. I thought about Flora every second of every minute of every day for about two years. If a minute passed when I did not think of her

I would have to then think about how I had not thought about her, thus then thinking about her.

I was only not thinking about what had happened when I was asleep, and I was blessed in that unlike some bereaved parents, I could sleep – it was waking up that was the problem. I would not actually have harmed myself, but I felt that if I could go to bed and not wake up it would be an end to my pain, a great relief. I did not want to live feeling as I did and at that time could not see that I would ever feel other than the way I did then. Life stretched before me like an endless, joyless desert. There was no consolation in anything at all.

Sleep offered a break but waking up was horrible – even before I opened my eyes the immediate realisation of Flora's death would descend on me as if it had just happened. My first and last waking thoughts were of her. Memories were painful as whenever I thought of her the realisation that she was dead followed with devastating immediacy.

The second year was worse than the first as it became apparent that having done all the anniversaries, birthdays and special occasions I would now have to do them again... and again... and again... The years projected relentlessly into the future and only death could end the suffering.

Christmas was to be dreaded and each year I would delay my shopping in the vain hope that if I made no preparations then it would not come. It was probably eight years before I could enjoy Christmas.

Easter was the time of Flora's anniversary, and whilst I could identify with Good Friday, my life held nothing of Easter's joy. In fact for several years I did not go to an Easter Sunday service, until invited to the First Communion of the grandson of a friend; tellingly, she was also a bereaved parent.

The emotional wound was deeper than I can describe, and yet the expectation of the population at large was that it was something that could be helped by going on holiday – some even suggested that it was a good time to find a job! They forgot that when you go on holiday you take with you baggage other than that contained in your suitcase, and as for finding a job, I could not contemplate anything new, in fact I could barely manage the familiar.

From the description I have given, which by no means covers the entirety of the devastation I felt, you will gather that the healing process was to be prolonged and painful, made more so by the fact that like any bereaved parent, I felt that if I let go the grief I would be losing Flora all over again, since grief was all I had left. **Kay Allen**

"Grief is like a long valley, a winding valley where any bend may reveal a totally new landscape . . . not every bend does. Sometimes the surprise is the opposite one; you are presented with exactly the same sort of country you thought you had left behind miles ago. That is when you wonder whether the valley isn't a circular trench. But it isn't". **C S Lewis**

How do you mend a broken heart,
when your reason for living has gone?
Where do you search for the healing you need,
when there is no one there?

Gill Hartley

Sometimes, I have come across poems that, although not related to the loss of child, or even the loss of a fellow being, still manage to capture the pain and sadness of loss. I am including the following poems for that reason as they speak so much of the bond between parent and child.

Cows

All evening the cows bellowed.
The valley moaned with their lowing,
seeping into the November woods
filling the purple dusk.
It was as though the trees wept.

And when the sky and the night and woods were one,
the darkness mourned with the cow's deep cry.
I walked by the edge of the sighing wood, and some one said,
"Their calves have been taken from them today."
And it was I, who wept.

Linden Saunders

White Rhino in Winter
And suddenly ... clamped on road side,
zooless - but ours for the viewing,
prehistoric pedestrian - pavement slab for hide,
blank blinkers stare seemingly - at nothing.

Handicapped horn bent towards winter earth,
the haunting whisper of captivated guide,
"She carried two calves for fourteen months,
- she lost them last week to a pride."

Mother's eyes on sun drenched winter evening.
Weighted monument in mourning.

Jan Moran Neil

I was driving along a country lane not far from our home. We had been experiencing extremely cold, frosty weather and it was a little foggy. It was beginning to clear a little and the sun was trying to break through. It made me think about the early days of our loss, when we feel lost and confused. But the sun is always there, even on days when we think we can't see it; it is there, giving us light, warmth and hope.

I am alone on this frozen lake,
no one seems to come near,
in places the ice is very thin,
perhaps that's the reason for their fear.

There's a cold sea fog surrounding me,
I hear voices but no one is there.
I hear laughter and conversation,
but no one knows I am here.

Sometimes, someone reaches out
across the frozen shore
and I warm to the touch of another's hand
the knowledge that somebody cares.

Gill Hartley

Unmade roads

Phone Call...
Some years begin with a prayer
or a wish on a new moon
others begin kingfisher blue
but end with hail.

One year began in April
a phone call in the afternoon.
That spring the ground sprouted nails.
Danielle Hope

When we lose a beloved child we are thrown into a totally unfamiliar landscape and many parents talk about their grief as a journey and the terrain as a road. I have used the description "unmade road" because that is exactly what it is. People love to tell us about the stages of grief, and that once we have worked through these stages, we will reach a point where we can accept what has happened to us. We will never do that. When we first lost Will I can remember saying over and over again that all I could see ahead of me was a grey and empty road. And as we do journey along it, we encounter pitfalls and setbacks.

From the outset I want to tell you that with the loss of your child or your children, you have embarked on the loneliest and longest of journeys. In many ways, it is a journey without an end. But as you travel along the lengthy road, you will find in yourself an inner strength you did not know was there. Incredibly, most of us do survive the death of our precious child. We may not want to, indeed we may contemplate suicide or wish we could die and be with our child. I know I did. But as time passes, you find ways to cope, ways of dealing with the lack of understanding you are almost certain to encounter. The pain does not go away and there will be times when it will be as raw and all consuming as it is right now.

The diagrams below show how others perceive us and how we actually are. In the first diagram, we are full of grief. In the second we are depicted as others tend to see us – we remain the same but our grief has diminished. The third diagram depicts how it really is for us. The grief remains the same but we have grown around it.

Searching
*Once again on this perilous path
as so many times in the past
facing the same uncertainties,
getting lost as before,
Each time stung by nettles,
bound up by the weeds,
tripped by sinuous roots and
brambles that tear at my clothes.
I fall into treacherous traps
the quicksand sets for me.
My hands are splintered
as I clamber across the
stiles determined to get in my way.
They are hard to climb
but go on I must.
I know this track leads nowhere
it is futile to keep coming back,
but I will return
for I have to believe
one day I'll find that clearing,
a place where the sun breaks through,
where wild flowers grow in abundance,
and I'm reunited with you.*

Gill Hartley

The belief that the first stage of our grief is shock, followed by denial and then numbness, is mistaken if only because these emotions do not come in set stages. These emotions can all come at once, together with guilt and misery. The numbness we can all identify with. We would not be able to live through our child's funeral were it not for numbness. Looking back on that time, it was as if I was 'on autopilot'. It was someone else, not me, who stood in the church staring at Will's coffin on the altar steps. It was someone else who talked with mourners at the reception after the service - maybe that was why some people found it necessary to comment how well I was doing and how brave I was.

In his inspiring book, "God of the Valley", Steve Griffiths relates how a friend told him that he believed denial to be a gift from God. Denial provides us with a safety net – we cannot absorb the magnitude of what has happened to us overnight. It takes time. A long time.

I saw a counsellor for a short time, not long after Will died, and when I told her what I had read in Steve's book, her reaction surprised me. "Oh no," she said, "You can't stay in denial. You must accept what has happened as soon possible". Unsurprisingly, it was not long after this that the counsellor and I parted company.

For me, one of the overriding emotions in those very early days was guilt. I felt I had let my son down. I should have been able to save him. How could I let my son die? I would lie awake, night after night after night, telling my husband it was my entire fault. I should have realised how serious it was. Why didn't I stop the medical team carrying out this or that procedure? I spent hours trying to rewrite it all, as if I could somehow turn it all round and bring Will back. I read many years ago that the saddest words in the English language are, "If only". How true. I tortured myself endlessly with the belief that it was I, and only I, who was ultimately to blame for my son's death, despite the reassurance of others that if the doctors didn't understand, how could I?

Although I was alone much of the time, occasionally well-meaning friends tried to persuade me to go out with them, to go shopping or maybe to a garden centre for a cup of tea. Knowing I felt lonely it probably seemed odd when I refused but what they could not appreciate was how unreal everything seemed. If I did consent to accompany a friend to a shop, I would view all that was going on around me as if I were looking through a glass screen. I could not understand how everyone was going about his or her daily lives as if nothing had happened. Didn't they understand? Didn't they know that the world was no longer the same place, that someone very precious was missing? I wanted to shout at everyone, "Don't you know that my son has died? How can you carry on as if everything is normal when it's not?"

It is much too easy in the early days of our grief to allow others to push us into doing things we really don't want to do. I felt that if I did not go along with some of the suggestions, it would be perceived as weakness on my behalf. I have many regrets about those foggy days. But of course we have no training. Our minds are in a state of total confusion and we don't seem to belong anywhere. We are totally lost.

What has happened to us can never be "acceptable" but what we do learn are ways of coping with our loss and to live with the pain the absence of our beloved child brings. We have to learn to shield ourselves from the thoughtless and hurtful comments from others, to try to hold on to the fact that they do not understand. And, because they feel the need to say something, come out with all the old clichés and platitudes that cause us anger and not comfort. One bereaved mother observed that she felt judged by others because they did not know what to do and they therefore asked questions such as, in my case, "Aren't you driving yet?" Then they could imply that once I got out and about again in the car, I would feel better. In this way they were attempting to provide a solution to our grief, when of course there isn't one.

In fact, I didn't drive for a long time because I felt I would be a risk to others on the road as my concentration was so poor. I also could not get in the car for a while because of all the associations with Will, but I could not explain that to anyone.

In Victor Frankl's book, "Man's Search for Meaning" he relates some of his experiences as a concentration camp prisoner and the psychological effects on the individual inmates. Frankl noted that *"We dislike talking about our experiences. No explanations are needed for those who have been inside, and the others will neither understand how we felt then or how we feel now."*

The following quotation from Marcel Proust says it all, I think.

There is no more ridiculous custom than the one that makes you express sympathy once and for all on a given day to a person whose sorrow will endure as long as his life. Such grief, felt in such a way is always present, it is never too late to talk about it, never repetitious to mention it again.

Marcel Proust

Gina Claye lost two of her young adult children, one to suicide and the second to illness. In the following poem she describes the feelings we have when our child or children die – that, "life was over". It all seemed pointless.

Yesterday
we shared a meal
opened a bottle

of wine, filled our days
together. Today I
cook for one

for something to do, scrape
much of it into the bin
uneaten. And tomorrow,

I have no plans for tomorrow.
Tell me, what
am I to do

with this leftover life?

Gina Claye

I love the sentiments expressed in the following poem which Kay Allen wrote for her daughter, Flora. We wonder in the early days of our loss whether we will ever feel able to enjoy life again and, as Kay says, untie the knots that bound us to our child. In time we realise that those threads will never be untied and we don't want them to be. What we do want is for the threads to loosen, so that we look back at the beautiful pattern our child created in our lives, without the pain of threads drawn so tightly that we can barely breathe.

Knots

How long will it take to untie
The knot in every thread
Spun over twenty years and more?
How long to unloose the tangles
That the years have wound around my heart?
Complex is the weave; and tightly bound
Each strand of love that holds me still to you.
Vivid and varied are the colours
Of the many-textured yarns of memory
That flow across the years of our yet short separation.
Year for year, my fingers pluck at each knot,
Until the nails break, and my finger ends grow raw.
Blood mingles with my tears.

In another twenty years shall I watch
Each colour and texture flowing free again,
Making of your life a new and richer cloth
Of deepest purple velvet night
Scattered with bright gold stars.   **Kay Allen**

We all have regrets over things we said or didn't say, things we might have done and didn't. After Will died, I spent agonising hours trying to make everything right again. It was like watching one of those documentaries when you know what the ending is going to be and you can't change it. I think Robert Frost's much loved poem captures these feelings well...

The Road Not Taken

Two roads diverged in a yellow wood,
And sorry I could not travel both
And be one traveller, long I stood
And looked down one as far as I could
To where it bent in the undergrowth;
Then took the other, as just as fair,
And having perhaps the better claim,
Because it was grassy and wanted wear;
Though as for that the passing there
Had worn them really about the same,
And both that morning equally lay

In leaves no step had trodden black.
Oh, I kept the first for another day!
Yet knowing how way leads on to way,
I doubted if I should ever come back.
I shall be telling this with a sigh
Somewhere ages and ages hence:
Two roads diverged in a wood, and I -
I took the one less travelled by,
And that has made all the difference.

Robert Frost

No lights are over the mesa,
The wind is hard and wild,
I stand at the darkened window
And cry like a child. **Sara Teasdale**

Gone...

I thought that I could learn to cope,
that life might yet begin again.
I would find other things to do
to help me face a future without you.

I set out bravely on this quest,
to comfort others in their grief,
perhaps if I could help them to survive
I'd keep the memory of you alive.

I did not know this path would be so steep
that I would stumble and fall back
into the comfort of my pain
and all my efforts be in vain.

For I do not have the strength to fight
the lack of understanding, or find the will,
to walk this endless road that leads nowhere
and live a life so cruelly stripped bare
of happiness and all that I held dear.

I cannot face a future without you.

Gill Hartley

Some parents see their children
After death.
In dreams.
Believe in signs -
Talk to them even.
I can't dream, can't talk, can't believe
That he is anything but gone.
And I wish I could
With all my heart.

Diane Shepherd

In the depths of your hopes and desires lies your secret
knowledge of the beyond:
And like seeds dreaming beneath the snow your heart
dreams of spring,
Trust the dreams, for in them is hidden the gate to eternity.

Kahlil Gibran. From "The Prophet"

I run a watercolour class in our village. The first Christmas after Will died, the group, knowing my love of gardening and poetry, bought me a little book of gardening poems. Amongst the poems about roses and flowers, I came across following poem. It was so unexpected, so powerful and so like the situation we had found ourselves in with Will, that I broke down in tears. I am including it because my reaction on reading it and the poem itself capture so well how life as we know it can change so abruptly and throw us into totally unfamiliar and traumatic circumstances.

Visiting Hour
In the pond of our new garden
were five orange stains, under
inches of ice. Weeks since anyone
had been there. Already by far
the most severe winter for years.
You broke the ice with a hammer.
I watched the goldfish appear,
blunt nosed and delicate.

Since then so much has taken place
to distance us from what we were.
That it should come to this.
Unable to hide the horror
in my eyes, I stand helpless
by your bedside and can do no more
than wish it were simply a matter
of smashing the ice and giving you air.
                                        Stewart Conn

Sad winds where your voice was;
Tears, tears where my heart was;
And ever with me,
Child, ever with me,
Silence where hope was.
        From Autumn by Walter De La Mare

Bereaved couples often deal differently with their grief. Men often need to compartmentalise their grief, something mothers are less able to do. It can be easy for the parents to misunderstand each other - the mother can think that her husband does not seem to care. And, because each parent has their own grief to deal with, it is often difficult to reach out to one another; you are both hurting too much. I think the following poem captures well the often unspoken grief of fathers.

I heard quite often "Men don't cry"
Though no one ever told me why,
So when I fell and skimmed a knee,
No one came to comfort me.

And when some bully boy at school
Would pull a prank so mean and cruel,
I'd quickly learn to turn and quip
"It doesn't hurt," and bite my lip.

So as I grew to reasoned years,
I learned to stifle any tears.
Though "Be a big boy" it began,
Quite soon I learned to "Be a man."

And I could play that stoic role
While storm and tempest wracked my soul.
No pain or setback could there be,
Could wrest one single tear from me.

Then one long night I stood nearby
And helplessly watched my son die,
And quickly found to my surprise
That all that tearless talk was lies.

And still I cry and have no shame,
I cannot play that "big boy" game
And openly without remorse
I let my sorrow take its course.

So those of you who can't abide
A man you've seen who's often cried,
Reach out to him with all your heart
As one whose life's been torn apart.
For men to cry when they can see
Their loss of immortality.
And tears will come in endless streams,
When mindless fate destroys their dreams.

Anonymous

Tears are the silent language of grief.

Voltaire

My husband, Edwin, wrote the following poem shortly after Will's death. It was the first poem Edwin had ever written and I am including it here because I think it is so beautiful and so heart-felt.

For Will

We had such hopes for you this year
to see you embark on your new career,
Ministry training to serve our Lord,
to become a vicar would be your reward.
But sadly this was not to be,
you were struck with a virus, so violently.

You lay in your bed and fought so hard,
so many visitors, and "get well" cards.
Wrapped in our love and Christ Church prayers,
a smile, a handshake with all you shared.
But despite all the equipment and medical care,
to which we clung in both hope and despair,
the strength, which sustained you during your life,
slipped slowly away through day and night.

When the last night we were called to your side.
the nurses and doctor stood by and cried.
Dear Carole and Jerry shared in our grief,
our last time with you so painfully brief.
You were at peace, we said goodbye
your spirit ascended to God on high.
As we stood by your bed, we knew we must
send you on to a new life with the Father we trust.
To be in service to our Lord,
we knew your true calling could not be ignored.

Now with you gone, our hearts are broken,
our grief, pain and sadness a token
of the love we shared for twenty-two years.
Unable now to stop shedding tears.
Keep safe, our son, until we meet
in Heaven with you and take our seat.
Together again for eternity,
once again a family.

"Loving together and forever, Dad."
Written by Edwin in memory of our dear son Will.

After Will died, I felt burdened by a sense of having to put on a brave face for everyone. I soon found that it did not help to be too honest and that it was much simpler to say "I'm fine, thank you." Even the most well intentioned people have a limited time to give you when you are grieving deeply. They have their own lives to lead and they need to move on. They are much happier to think that you are feeling "better", as they then feel comfortable when they stretch out the time between their phone calls or visits to you. They cannot really be expected to understand how far

35

reaching and never ending our grief is. No matter how far along this unmade road we travel, it will always be uphill.

weep
I weep
ooze slowly
salty red wounds
weep weeping willows
winter willows wept sore
winter seepage – wept wept raw
wounding warring sometime roaring
wept tears and tears, tears and tears I weep
I am one acquainted with grief - like you.

Jan Moran Neil

The following poem by Ella Wilcox captures so well the feeling of waking each day to the realisation that sleep has been an escape from reality and that nothing has changed, our child is no longer here...

God pity her when from her dream Elysian
She wakes to see the empty crib, and weep;
Knowing her joy was but a sleeper's vision,
Tread lightly – let her sleep.

Ella Wheeler Wilcox
From Ashes of Life

Love has gone and left me and the days are all alike;
Eat I must, and sleep I will, and would that night were here!
But ah, to lie awake and hear the slow hours strike!
Would that it were day again - with twilight near!

Love has gone and left me and I don't know what to do;
This or that or what you will is all the same to me;
But all the things that I begin I leave before I'm through,
There's little use in anything as far as I can see.

Love has gone and left me, and the neighbours knock and borrow,
And life goes on forever like the gnawing of a mouse,
And to-morrow and to-morrow and to-morrow and to-morrow
There's this little street and this little house.

Edna St Vincent Millay

It is almost impossible to make decisions when we are grieving deeply. We moved into our present home a year before Will became ill and were in the throes of having it extended when he was admitted to hospital. Will was transferred to a hospital in Leicester after three days in intensive care in our local hospital and we stayed in a motel near the hospital for six weeks. When we returned home without him, the house was in chaos and we stayed with friends until the final works were completed. When we did return home, trying to make decisions as to what wallpaper or curtain fabric we wanted was almost impossible for me. Fortunately a cousin, who is very clever at interior design, came to the rescue.

Sorrow

Sorrow like a ceaseless rain
Beats upon my heart.
People twist and scream in pain,
Dawn will find them still again;
This has neither wax nor wane,
Neither stop nor start.

People dress and go to town;
I sit in my chair.
All my thoughts are slow and brown:
Standing up or sitting down
Little matters, or what gown
Or what shoes I wear.

Edna St Vincent Millay

The absence of our child is almost impossible to bear. We cannot believe that they are not coming home, that we will not see them again. We know deep within our consciousness that they have died but our minds and hearts cannot and will not accept it. We truly believe we are losing our minds, the sense of unreality is overwhelming and we want to rewrite it all, make everything as it was before.

Absence

I visited the place where we last met.
Nothing was changed, the gardens were well tended,
The fountains sprayed their usual steady jet;
There was no sign that anything had ended.
And nothing to instruct me to forget.

The thoughtless birds that shook out of the trees,
Singing an ecstasy I could not share,
Playing cunning in my thoughts.
Surely in these pleasures there could not be a pain to bear
Or any discord shake the level breeze.

It was because the place was just the same
That made your absence seem a savage force,
For under all the gentleness there came an earthquake tremor:
Fountain, birds and grass
Were shaken by my thinking of your name.

Elizabeth Jennings

Once Seen

Once I could see the rising sun,
On the fields that sparkled with dew.
The shades of green on all the trees,
And the sea and the sky oh so blue.

Once I could see the flowers in bloom,
Their colours so vivid and bright,
Like the sun when it sets in the evening,
And the moon and the stars every night.

Once I could see the Blackbird sing,
The Robin, the Thrush and the Lark,
And the wise old Owl with its great big eyes,
Who hoots every night when its dark.

Once I could see your face so bright,
Like the sun which shines in the skies.
The smile on your face as I touched your hand,
And the look of love in your eyes.

Once I could see the snowflakes fall,
With their touch as soft as a kiss.
And the raindrops that fall from the heavens
Are my tears for these things that I miss.

Brian Saunders

Dirge without Music

I am not resigned to the shutting away
of loving hearts in the hard ground.
So it is, and so it will be,
for so it has been, time out of mind:
Into the darkness they go, the wise and the lovely.
Crowned with lilies and with laurel they go;
but I am not resigned.

Lovers and thinkers, into the earth with you.
Be one with the dull, the indiscriminate dust.
A fragment of what you felt, of what you knew,
A formula, a phrase remains,—but the best is lost.

The answers quick and keen,
the honest look, the laughter, the love,—
They are gone. They are gone to feed the roses.
Elegant and curled
Is the blossom. Fragrant is the blossom.
I know. But I do not approve.
More precious was the light in your eyes
than all the roses in the world.

Down, down, down into the darkness of the grave
Gently they go, the beautiful, the tender, the kind;
Quietly they go, the intelligent, the witty, the brave.
I know. But I do not approve. And I am not resigned.

Edna St Vincent Millay

Into my heart an air that kills
From yon far country blows
What are those blue remembered hills,
What spires, what farms are those?

That is the land of lost content,
I see it shining plain,
The happy highways where I went
And cannot come again.

Houseman

I was talking with a friend who is an experienced bereavement counsellor, working specifically with children and bereaved families. When I said that I had a constant ache in the pit of my stomach, she looked at me and said, "Gill, that's a broken heart". This ache will never go away and there are times when the grief and sadness overwhelm us. I sometimes feel that it is almost as if I am expected to "pretend" Will never existed in order to make others feel more comfortable. I have voiced those thoughts when I have been in company and there has been what almost amounts to a refusal to mention Will. He deserves my grief and I know that I will grieve for him until the day I die. In his book, A Grief Observed, CS Lewis says,

> *"If a mother is mourning not for what she has lost but for what her dead child has lost, it is a comfort to believe that the child has not lost the end for which it was created. A comfort to the God-aimed, eternal spirit within her. But not to her motherhood. The specifically maternal happiness must be written off. Never, in any place or time, will she have her son on her knees, or bathe him or tell him a story, or plan for his future, or see her grandchild."*

From Kahlil Gibran's much loved book, **The Prophet**...

And a woman who held a baby against her bosom said,

Speak To Us of Children!

And he said:
They are the sons and daughters of Life's longing for itself.
They come through you but not from you,
And though they are with you yet they belong not to you.
You may give them your love but not your thoughts,
For they have their own thoughts.
You may house their bodies but not their souls,
For their souls dwell in the house of tomorrow,
which you cannot visit, not even in your dreams.
You may strive to be like them,
but seek not to make them like you.
For life goes not backward nor tarries with yesterday.

Kahlil Gibran

Washing Day

That day...
when I pegged your clothes
onto the line,
Yours, and your father's, mine.
His shirts; your tee-shirts,
Underpants: large Y fronts for your father
Smaller medium size boxer shorts for you.
The sleeveless vests you liked to wear.
Assorted socks: yours, your father's, mine.
Such an ordinary everyday thing to do.

How could I have known,
that bright sunny morning,
I would never do it again?

Gill Hartley

No matter how hard we try, the hopelessness of our situation overwhelms us at times and we feel we cannot cope, that we do not have the strength to go on....

But, somehow, we do. We find in ourselves an inner strength we were not aware of before and we go on because we loved our child. Much as I dislike the cliché, "Will would want you to…" I know that it is true. Will would want me to go on living. And, somehow, I will. We have a saying in TCF, "One step at a time and remember to breathe."

One Step Forward… many steps back.
This is a mountainous road,
such steep hills to climb,
I think I'm nearing the summit,
then I'm faced with another ravine.

A sudden memory,
a thoughtless remark,
a young man who
resembles you,
causes me to lose my grip,
and again I fall.

I get back on my feet,
determined to do it this time,
but the burden is too heavy
and I break down and cry.

I think I have made some progress
I have conquered some of the slopes,
But my feet are heavy
and this path is rough,
and I cannot hold onto my hopes.

I pray, in time I'll get stronger
learn how to carry this pain,
if I keep one foot
in front of the other,
my efforts might not be in vain.

Gill Hartley

Sometimes you will fall under your Cross,
Jesus did – three times.

Brother Roger

Edwin, Will, and me

I took the photo of Will and Edwin when we were on holiday together in Ireland in 2003. Will took the photo of me, on the same occasion, and somehow managed to put the three of us together to produce the above picture. This explains why the shadows differ.
I love this photo and it hangs in the hall at home – a treasured memory of happier times...

Diane

Empty rooms and silent phones

Contact
Oh, I have been ringing you
from all the phone boxes I know.
Danielle Hope

I still have Will's phone number on my mobile phone - even when I bought a new one I transferred his number, along with all the others, to my new phone. And although I use his room as my office, the cupboards remain full of his clothes and belongings. All my work on the computer still appears under the heading, "Mum's" from when I had to replace Will's old computer and transfer all the files to the new one.

I often think of Will's room in the hospital and in my mind I can see it clearly. For a long time I could see the faces of all the doctors and nurses involved in caring for him and, although I would still recognise them were I to meet them now, the mental images have faded. His room always seemed to be full of people – he was in intensive care so there was always a nurse present – and we had regular visitors, many from our church. We had such wonderful support from our church members when Will was in hospital, I do not know how we would have coped without them. Given the fact that Will had been transferred to a hospital in Leicester, travelling to visit us meant a journey of around one and half hours. Yet we did have visitors and their support was invaluable. It never occurred to me that the support would not be there when we returned home. But it wasn't and the shock of realising that we were now largely on our own was hard to bear.

We were unable to return to our own home, as it was in the throes of being extended when Will became unwell and I could not face the chaos the house was in.

A married couple from work kindly invited us to stay with them and so, after leaving my cousin's home in Nottingham, it was to their home we returned, a few days after Will died. Soon after we moved in with them, the husband returned to Mongolia where he was working and because Judy, his wife, was also working, I spent much of my time alone, especially once Edwin had returned to work.

I could not do anything. When my husband went back to work, a few weeks after Will's death, I would get up, dress and go downstairs. Then I would sit, for hour after hour, just staring into space. I longed for more people to come and see me but although some did come, visits were infrequent. I longed for the phone to ring, to speak with someone and often phoned help lines during the day. The need to talk about Will, and what had happened, was overpowering.

Well has it been said that there is no grief like the grief which does not speak.

Henry Wadsworth Longfellow

My niece lent me a Game Boy and I would fiddle with that, but my hands were so shaky that I struggled with even the lowest level of the game. My sister gave me some wool to knit a scarf and I would sometimes pick that up and knit a few rows.

But for most of the time I just sat. I remember sitting in the same chair every morning and staring at the hand-made rug on the floor. It had a cross on it – a happy mistake I think, and I would stare at the cross, trying to understand why God had seemingly deserted me. I could not even put the kettle on to make myself a cup of tea and if Edwin had not taken over all the cooking, I would have starved. I have never been a heavyweight but my weight fell to six and a half stone – much of the weight already lost during the six weeks Will was in Intensive Care. How could I eat when my son was being fed via a feeding tube? My stomach rejected any food I tried to swallow and I was often physically sick.

When Edwin and I returned home after losing Will, we were both physically and emotionally drained. We lived on convenience food for weeks, although much of the time my appetite was so poor that I could happily have starved anyway. That is where friends can help and if they offer to bring you some food or do some shopping for you, do accept their offer. You need all the help you can get. It was some time before I could prepare a meal and, even now, Edwin does most of the cooking.

Catastrophic loss takes a toll on our health. My osteopath likened my loss of Will and the effects on my health to being hit by a double-decker bus.

In Barbara Rosof's excellent book "The Worst Loss", she tells of a bereaved mother who was told by a friend that if she had sustained physical injuries as severe as her emotional injury, she would be in intensive care. And no one would expect someone in intensive care to carry out every day tasks and carry on with normal life.

Will used to tease me and call me a "silver surfer" when it came to using the Internet to buy anything. I wish he could see me now. I now buy most of my clothes and Edwin's via the Internet as I still find shopping stressful.

Only the silence of these empty rooms
after the sudden sound of your leaving,
a sharp sound like the edge of a knife
striking stony ground.

Memories of laughter trickle into draughty space.
Doors bang, monotonous, one by one,
against you.

Absence creeps along the walls.

Elsewhere drifts of melody,
the blue china rattle of tea-cups;
running water; radio voices; rain.

Nearer, my nail scratchings along the page.
This long white page.

Pat Sentinella

When I told my mother I was pregnant, she commented, "You'll never be alone again." Now, I remember her words and reflect how ironic they seem. I had often read how grief isolates but it is only when we are faced with such immense loss, that we can appreciate the truth behind those words.

Because of the magnitude of our loss, it is impossible for others to understand and many parents experience the loneliness and isolation we endured.

I have lost both my parents, aunts, uncles, cousins and close friends. I grieved for them of course, but not in the way I grieve for my son. To be fair, people can only measure grief by their own experience but the loss of a child is immeasurable. When our child or children die, we lose our past, our present and our future. Our dreams are crushed and the future as we envisaged it is changed forever. We are programmed to lose our parents one day, perhaps even our partners. But we do not expect to outlive our children; it is the wrong order of things. The grief we feel for our children will never diminish, it will be with us until we ourselves die.

Because our children will always be younger than us, their birthdays will always be poignant. Edwin takes a day off work for Will's birthday and we try to go somewhere quiet, to think about him. The first year we made the mistake of going to a garden centre for lunch. It was not a success and we picked the wrong day, as the following poem describes.

Ageing

Today is your birthday
to mark the day we lunch
at a garden centre
frequented by you and I.

We had not realised
today is set aside
for retired folk, like me,
But unlike me.

No vegetarian choice,
far too adventurous
for OAP day.
We settle for jacket potatoes,
everyone else has
meat and two veg.

In the window seat:
a gentleman with few teeth, if any.
Ordering a sausage sandwich,
he smothers it in salt,
I try to avert my eyes,
each time he attempts a bite.

At the next table:
two ladies,
one wears, "fun" wool
white hat and scarf.
Her friend has a serviette tucked
under her chin.
Again I am drawn like a magnet
to watch as they so-o slow-l-y eat.

I can almost hear you say,
"No one needs that do they, Mum?"

No, Will, no one needs that.
I tell your father,
"I don't want to get old"
And that, my darling,
you will never fear,
for you will always be young.

Gill Hartley

49

I think we learn to accept that, by our very circumstances, we will feel isolated in our grief. We cannot really expect others to understand and we wouldn't want them to suffer the devastating loss we have experienced to give them that understanding.

As Compassionate Friends have proved, the only way we can find the understanding and companionship we crave, is in the company of others in the same heart-breaking position as ourselves. And, even then, there will be times when even our friends within TCF cannot be there for us. We each have our own precious child or children and the loss of a unique relationship to mourn; none of us can honestly say, "I know how you feel."

At any gathering of members from Compassionate Friends, you will hear endless stories from parents, relating the hurtful and thoughtless comments, the awful clichés. There is always laughter at such gross misunderstanding and ineptitude. But beneath the laughter there is pain.

The following poems reflect the anger and disappointment we feel when we realise how alone we are and how others just cannot comprehend our pain.

You may my glories and my state depose,
But not my griefs. Still I am king of those.
Shakespeare: Richard II

Why not ask me?
I hear it again and again,
one friend asked another how I had been.
How hard, really, would it be
to pick up the phone and just ask me?
Genesse Gentry

This poem by Tony Turner captures the "crossing the road" syndrome perfectly.

Links

After a marathon of pain
four weeks ago today he died
and though it feels as if one side
of me has gone
I must go on.

Friends cross the road to miss me
or hide behind the supermarket shelves.
Phone calls have dwindled
into careful letters.
Those who can't avoid me
avoid him like the plague
as though he never was.

I need friends
to make links in a new pattern
to talk to me as if I were still me
and not diseased,
to let me talk
and to remember him.

Tony Turner

When a person is born we rejoice, and when they're married we jubilate, but when they die we try to pretend nothing has happened.

Margaret Mead

It is easy to love the people far away. It is not always easy to love those close to us. It is easier to give a cup of rice to relieve hunger than to relieve the loneliness and pain of someone unloved in our own home. Bring love into your home for this is where our love for each other must start.

Mother Teresa of Calcutta

I found the following poem very poignant, as the thought of the mother in the poem, taking blankets to her son in the cemetery, locked into my memories of tucking Will into his cot when he was a baby, worrying he might be cold in the night...

I heard
tell
of Mrs Kelly
seen
often
in Derry City's
cemetery
on a cold night
with blankets
to keep
her son
warm
and know now
I have not
remembered
enough

Chris Agee

Please stop trying to console me,
Don't tell me there's a reason I'm still here.
My son is dead and that is all that matters,
He was my life and all that I held dear.
Gill Hartley

I use Will's room as my office. I sit surrounded by all his books, photographs and posters. His cupboards still contain all his clothes. I have not yet found the courage or real desire to move anything. There are books he was in the middle of reading, old family slides he was so meticulously sorting through and filing. It is still, in every sense, Will's room but without his physical presence.

My husband had a couple of weeks off last summer and we had promised ourselves that, weather permitting, we would make some effort to sort out some of the items in the garden cabin, particularly Will's university books, which I felt we should offer to the university library.

We didn't get very far. I returned from my creative writing group one morning to find that Edwin had made a start on the room. He had erected a temporary table and on this he had placed several boxes, which I began to unpack.

Within half an hour I crumbled. I could not do it. I could not sort through Will's possessions, knowing that he would never be doing it himself. It felt wrong. It felt like betrayal. It would be admitting he is never coming back and I realise I am not ready to do that. The question is, will I ever be? Perhaps, if we had surviving children or close family to pass some of his things on to it would be less painful.

And it doesn't stop there. What do we do with all the family heirlooms? Who will want all the "treasures" I have kept, such as Will's first shoes and school exercise books, when I am no longer here? I sometimes think it can all wait until I am with Will and then someone else can do it. People are quick to tell us that we must not turn our child's room into a shrine and that we should "move on". I wrote about this for the Compassionate Friends journal Compassion and many parents wrote to say how they had coped with their child's belongings. Some felt like me and had not been able to sort anything out, finding it too painful, often many years after the death of their child.

Diane Shepherd, whose son died in a car accident in 1998, told me how she had bought a large wooden trunk in which to put anything of Dan's she wished to keep. She also makes scrapbooks, into which she puts photographs, mementos and poems she has collected over the years and as these books become full, they too find their way into this precious chest of memories. I thought it was a wonderful idea and searched for a chest to put into our room. Eventually I found a beautiful old pine chest on EBay and bought it. It sits under the eaves in our bedroom. But we have yet to put any of Will's things into it. I am sure there will come a day when I will find the strength to sort through Will's possessions and put anything we want to keep into this lovely old chest. Edwin and I both said how much Will would have loved the chest in his room when he was well and living at home with us. It would not have taken him long to fill it!

It
never
gets done
it sits
on the desk
covered in dust

the notebook
of "Memories"
I'm unable
to face

Chris Agee

The following poem was written by Gina Claye after she met with a bereaved mother who wanted to cry over her son's jacket but her family thought she shouldn't after, "all that time".

Don't let them tell you how to grieve
Though it's the same journey for all
there is no one way through.
Others may do it differently.
Let them. If you don't like
what they're saying, get them to leave.
Don't let anyone tell you how to grieve.

So what if you house is a mess.
Leave it. Tomorrow you just might
need to wring hell out of a dishcloth
or beat up a rug or two.
Never mind any raised eyebrows,
go by how you feel.
Don't let them tell you how to grieve.

Sit in the garden for hours drinking tea.
Dead head one rose.
Talk to the weeds if you want to.
Tell them it's their turn tomorrow,
whenever that is.

Let the grass grow under your feet.
Don't let them tell you how to grieve.

Don't do a big shop-up just
because you ought to. Order a pizza,
or heat up one of the unknown
objects lurking in the freezer.
Hug a bowl of custard. Have tomatoes
On toast for breakfast, lunch and tea.
Don't let them tell you how to grieve.

Ignore advice to pull yourself together.
Sit in the dark or light a candle.
It's OK to cry, to remember.
Wear his old sweater; let it hug you.
Sob over his jacket if it's what you need.
Sink a brandy, or two, or three.
Don't let them tell you how to grieve.

Refuse that kindly meant invitation
to get you out again.
If you don't want to go, say so.
Friends may mutter, shake their heads.
Don't take any notice. Let them.
They don't know exactly how you feel.
They're not the ones who've been bereaved.
Don't let them tell you how to grieve.

Gina Claye

We do learn over time to put on a public face. My niece tragically lost her first husband and baby in a car accident and told me that she would force herself to go into her son's nursery to make herself cry before she left for work. She was afraid that if she did not get some of the pain out, she might break down in tears at work. I could identify with that.

The tears streamed down, and I let them flow as freely as they
would, making a pillow of them for my heart. On them it rested.

St Augustine of Hippo

55

Some years before Will died; one of our two dogs collapsed and died of heart failure. His sudden death came as shock. The next day, shopping in a local supermarket, I found myself in tears. The reaction of those around me was an experience I would rather forget. People edged past me as if I had some contagious disease and when I asked for help carrying my shopping to my car, the assistant walked about two yards ahead of me. The experience left me with a fear of breaking down in public and after Will died, I tried to avoid situations that might provoke tears. But that is not easy, as the following poem describes so well.

Unforewarned

If you're grieving
and enduring
the insistent interface with life,
it's not the big dates that defeat you,
birthdays, deathdays,
you see those coming and you build your shield,
rehearse the grief so many times within your mind,
that, on the day, you just feel emptiness,
not pain.
What pierce straight through
that careful primed defence
are little things,
the spindly arrows of the nondescript;
a profile glimpsed, a snatch of song,
some tiny aching echo from another time,
which catch you quite unprepared
and bring you to your knees.

It makes you see
why execution by a thousand cuts
is so much crueller than the axe,

and leaves you fearful
of unanticipated slices
to come.

Jill Wallis

These poems describe so well how we have to hide our feelings in order to make others feel comfortable.

LIFE has dark secrets; and the hearts are few
That treasure not some sorrow from the world
A sorrow silent, gloomy, and unknown,
Yet colouring the future from the past.
We see the eye subdued, the practised smile,
The word well weighed before it pass the lip,
And know not of the misery within:

Letitia Elizabeth Landen

We Wear the Mask

We wear the mask that grins and lies,
It hides our cheeks and shades our eyes -
This debt we pay to human guile;
With torn and bleeding hearts we smile
And mouth with myriad subtleties,
Why should the world be over-wise,
In counting all our tears and sighs?
Nay, let them only see us, while
We wear the mask.
We smile, but oh great Christ, our cries
To Thee from tortured souls arise.
We sing, but oh the clay is vile
Beneath our feet, and long the mile,
But let the world dream otherwise,
We wear the mask!

Paul Laurence Dunbar

It is not good for us to have to conceal our grief. I found that having to swallow my tears in front of others, led to me finding it harder and harder to release the tears, even when I was alone.

Loss

If dislodged
like water in Archimedes' bath
it flows over the edge.

Loss cannot be compressed
and when frozen
like ice is bigger.

Danielle Hope

We look through gloom and storm-drift
Beyond the years:
The soul would have no rainbow
Had the eyes no tears.

John Vance Cheney

Heart Less

My life has fallen apart,
I am like a broken doll,
pieces of me are scattered
and I cannot find them all.

I need someone to help me
search for some of the parts.
Many of them will never be found,
they are lost, far in the past.

I do know where my heart is -
deep in the ground with you, my son,
but so much else is missing too,
like happiness and your love.

My memories are so fragile,
I fear I will lose them too,
if I don't try to recall
every moment spent with you.

Some of the pieces are shattered.
and can never be repaired:
my role as mother to you
and the future we will never share.

58

I pray I can find someone,
who cares enough to help me,
glue together a semblance
of the person I used to be.

Then I can don my armour,
smile and remember to laugh,
and outwardly be like anyone else,
except I am missing a heart.

Gill Hartley

Unspoken...

Dear Friend: Please put it behind you;
let go for a while.
You're too lost in mourning;
lighten up, try to smile.
I know it's a tragedy,
I know how you must feel,
but you must get through it,
move on, so you'll heal.
I just can't stand
to see you in pain.
I know if you try
you'll be happy again.

Dear Friend: The person you still
Want me to be
is gone, locked away
and I don't have the key.
I'm really not choosing
to be like this,
but my life is pure feeling,
clenching me like a fist.
When I venture out strongly,
the pain wraps me still,
colours my actions,
saps at my will.
So please don't give up,
though I'm hopeless and lost,
our friendship's true value
reflects in its costs.

Genesse Gentry

59

When the grief takes hold...

It'll happen on the train.
It'll happen on the bus.
It'll happen anytime.
It might happen over
And over again.

It'll get me when it wants to.
It'll get me all the while
And there's not a lot I can do.

Laura Samson

Time heals nothing – which should make us the better able to minister. There may be griefs beyond the reach of solace, but none worthy of the name that does not set free the springs of sympathy. Blessed are they that comfort, for they too have mourned, may be more likely the human truth.

Peter De Vries

When our son was first in hospital and we became aware of how serious his condition was, I remember hurling my bible across the room and telling God that I could not live without Will and did not even want to try.

One of the saddest aspects of losing our son is that we will never be grandparents or see our son achieve his dreams. However much we try to hold on to the hope that we will see Will again one day, it does not take away the pain of having to live the rest of our lives here without him. As my husband said recently, "I sometimes feel as if we are just marking time." I so often feel like that.

Changing

I find it hard to listen,
when people relate their woes,
I want say,
"Is that all? Get real."
but it's not their fault -
it's me.
My patience has deserted me,
I'm not the way I was before.
Whereas before I said "Yes"
it's simpler now to say "No".
I do not socialise these days,
it's easier to be alone,
than feel the need to apologise
and justify my grief.

Somehow I must deal with
the anger that I feel,
this feeling of utter frustration
for there's nothing I can do
to alter what has happened,
there is no one to blame.
The world is as it's always been
that is what makes it so hard,
for me nothing is normal,
I am angry,
because you have died.

Gill Hartley

Despair

I am in despair,
sick with longing for you,
I don't know what to do with myself,
and so few people seem to care.
The phone rarely rings these days,
no one asks me how I am,
I'm just expected to get on with my life,
pack you away in the past.

Gill Hartley

I've lived to bury my desires,
And see my dreams corrode with rust;
Now all that's left are fruitless fires
That burn my empty heart to dust

Alexander Pushkin

"There is nothing that can replace the absence of someone dear to
us, and one should not even attempt to do so. One must simply hold
out and endure it. It is wrong to say that God fills the emptiness.
God in no way fills it but much more leaves it precisely unfilled and
thus helps us preserve -- even in pain -- the authentic relationship.
Further more, the more beautiful and full the remembrances, the
more difficult the separation. But gratitude transforms the torment
of memory into silent joy. One bears what was lovely in the past not
as a thorn but as a precious gift deep within, a hidden treasure of
which one can always be certain."

Dietrich Bonhoeffer

At times life seems so normal...

Last night friends came to supper,
we laughed and talked
life seemed almost normal,
I was smiling when our friends said, "Goodnight"

But, once we are alone again,
reality rears its head,
Now, I sleep in a four-poster bed,
surrounded by curtains of grief and despair.

When I close my eyes I still see you
lying helpless in your hospital room,
dreading the endless night to come
when sleep eludes and we are not there.

Eventually I fall into restless sleep,
and when I waken, there's a beat -
a second or two, before I'm aware
that a new day has dawned, still without you.

Gill Hartley

The following poem by Shakespeare, shows that feeling misunderstood was as common with bereaved parents in Shakespeare's time as it is today. And it says so much about the empty room and the emptiness we feel in the absence of a much loved child.

Grief fills the room up of my absent child,
Lies in his bed, walks up and down with me,
Puts on his pretty looks, repeats his words,
Remembers me of all his gracious parts,
Stuffs out his vacant garments with his form;
Then have I reason to be fond of grief?
Fare you well: had you such a loss as I,
I could give better comfort than you do.

Shakespeare: King John

Friends

The friend who can be silent with us in a moment of
despair or confusion,
Who can stay with us in an hour of grief and bereavement,
who can tolerate not knowing...not healing, not
curing...that is a friend who cares.

Henri Nouwen

In those early days, because people did not know what to do or say, I was often left alone. It was around this time that my niece phoned to tell me about an organisation that soon became my lifeline. She asked me if I had heard of a national support group called, The Compassionate Friends (TCF). She went on to say that within TCF there was a special group for parents who had lost an only child. Later that day, I picked up the phone and rang the number my niece had given me – the number of TCF helpline. I managed to stutter out my reason for phoning and my garbled message was met with warmth and understanding. The TCF helpline is manned by bereaved parents and it is often the first time that a bereaved parent will speak with someone who truly understands their pain. TCF became a lifeline for my husband as well as for me and I can honestly say that I do not know how I would have survived without their love and support.

It was the day, my son,
When I knew you would die,
It was the day I asked Simon to pray for you.
It was the day he said, "and for Billy"
It was the first day of
The Compassionate Friends.

Joe Lawley – TCF founding parent.

A Story of Compassion

The Compassionate Friends was founded in Coventry in 1969 and is now a worldwide organisation, with chapters in the United States, Canada, Australia, New Zealand, South Africa, Spain and Malta, to name but a few.

It all began in 1968, in the Intensive Care Unit of the Coventry and Warwickshire Hospital, where an eleven-year-old boy, Kenneth, lay dying from injuries sustained in an accident. When his parents, Iris and Joe Lawley, invited the young assistant chaplain, the Reverend Simon Stephens, to pray with them for Kenneth, he suggested that they also pray for another child who lay dying in the same hospital, Billy Henderson. When the two children died within a few days of each other, Iris Lawley suggested to her husband that they send flowers to Billy Henderson's funeral. The two couples subsequently met and found much solace in sharing their grief with each other. In Joe Lawley's own words, *"Together, we were all able to accept, for the first time, the words used by many well-meaning friends, rejected almost universally by parents who have lost a beloved child — "I understand." We did understand, all four of us, and, in the immensity of our grief (and in reality is there any other tragedy of quite this enormity?), we all suffered together."*

Observing what a strength the two families were to each other, and that they were able to help one another in a way no one else could, Simon Stephens asked the two couples if they would consider working with other bereaved parents. The initial meeting took place in a room in the very hospital where the two children had died. There were six people present at that first meeting, including Simon Stephens and, from this small gathering in January 1969, The Society of the Compassionate Friends was born. Now called The Compassionate Friends (TCF) the organisation celebrated its 40th anniversary in October with a National Gathering at Bosworth Hall in Warwickshire, not far from Coventry where the organisation began.

I can honestly say that I am not sure I would have found the courage to go on with my life without the support of TCF and the wonderful new friends we have made through them. Our circle of friends is now quite different from that which existed before the death of our son.

When I think of TCF, I am reminded of Helen Keller, the extraordinary blind and deaf writer and speaker. She once spoke movingly of how the bereaved were not alone, that when it seemed their sorrow was too great to bear, they could think of the great family of the heavy hearted into which their grief had given them entrance. Then, she believed, they would feel about them this great family's arms, their sympathy, their understanding.

"Believe me," she said, "When you are most unhappy, that there is something for you to do in the world. So long as you can sweeten another's pain, life is not in vain."

I felt almost immediately after Will's death that my only hope of survival was to try and help others in a similar situation. I did not know at the time in which direction this thought would take me but knew it was something that would happen when the time was right. I think many of us feel this but a word of caution here; don't try to do too much, too soon. Looking back now I can see that I tried too hard sometimes, pushing my own emotions deeper and deeper inside. We need time for ourselves, to give ourselves some kindness and understanding. We have been deeply wounded and it doesn't take us long to realise that very few people, unless they too have experienced such devastating loss, can relate to our pain.

Grief knits two hearts in closer bonds than happiness ever can; and common sufferings are far stronger links than common joys.

Alphonse de Lamartine

To One In Sorrow

Let me come in where you are weeping, friend,
And let me take your hand.
I, who have known a sorrow such as yours,
Can understand.
Let me come in - I would be very still
Beside you in your grief.
I would not bid you cease your weeping, friend,
Tears bring relief.
Let me come in - I would only breathe a prayer,
And hold your hand,
For I have known a sorrow such as yours,
And understand.

Grace Noll Crowell

Sue White, whose son, Paul, died in a car accident twelve years ago at the age of eighteen, describes the special friendship they formed with another couple from Compassionate Friends. A friendship that began in the very early days of their loss.

TCF brought me the friendship that helped me to survive. Linda was the very first mother to contact me and we quickly progressed from a letter to a telephone call to meeting in person. That very first meeting lasted for five hours and Linda and I talked about our boys and shared photographs; we even shared the newspaper cuttings about the boys' deaths.

Once we had met and begun talking constantly on the telephone, we decided it would be nice for the men to meet as well, so we arranged to go out for a meal together. There were many comments from others that it may be too upsetting and we should not make friends with other bereaved parents. I am sure that family and friends really believed they were thinking of us; they wanted us to get better and for life to continue as it had when Paul was alive.

They had no understanding that life as it had been for us had ended. One of the most important people in our lives had gone and had taken the people we were with him.

It is so sad that our friends and family really only want the people they knew back and have little comprehension that it is impossible. I believe that is why bereaved parents see so many friends and, sometimes, family members disappear from their lives.

Since that first meeting, all four of us have been the closest of friends. We have been together at Christmas and on holidays. In those early years, we would talk about our feelings at losing our boys and share private thoughts and fears. It became a really comfortable relationship, a unique friendship in that we had no shared history.

Our friendship was forged when each of us was frozen in pain and the world, for us, had stopped. We found the comfort and courage we needed to take those first steps into a world that had changed almost beyond recognition. And we took those first steps together.

*We have picked each other up so many times. We have laughed
and had fun and tears have thread themselves throughout our new
lives, until we are made of them and yet still look a solid form!*

*Twelve years on, we are still close friends who enjoy spending a
lot of time together. We no longer need to talk constantly of our loss
– it is there running throughout our friendship and not lessened by
the fun, laughter or the joys in life.*

Sue White's heartening story of an enduring friendship forged through
tragedy is true of many parents from TCF. There is a bond and
understanding that bereaved parents find it difficult to find elsewhere. As
someone put it, "We speak the same language."

My husband Edwin and I attended our first gathering of bereaved
parents in November 2006, ten months after Will died. This particular
gathering had been organised by Rita Henshaw who, together with Barry
Bridges, had initiated what they called the Childless Parents group within
TCF. We found it a great comfort to be with other parents who had
suffered a similar loss to our own and we met with nothing but kindness
and understanding.

Since then we have attended other gatherings and although there are
times when our emotions are stretched to the limit, we have both felt
strengthened by the experience. The hardest part for us has been returning
home and being surrounded again by a society that cannot comprehend
our grief.

I realise that these gatherings are not for everyone, some parents find
them overwhelming and I can understand that. But for us, they help.

*What we have done for ourselves alone dies with us; what
we have done for others and the world remains and is
immortal.* **Albert Pike**

It has often been suggested to me that by belonging to TCF I am
somehow keeping my grief alive. Indeed, I was told by a friend who
herself had lost a baby some years ago, that, I should not even think of
joining TCF because I would only hear other people's sad stories and that
would make me feel worse. In fact, I found that in a seemingly perverse
way, learning of others losses brought a kind of comfort to me, the

69

knowledge I was not alone, and, more importantly, the realisation that if other parents had survived such a tragedy, maybe I could too.

I am including this excellent article by Eva Lager, a bereaved mother who lives in Australia and the author of an excellent book, "Knowing Why Changes Nothing". I can so identify with all that she says, and I am sure many other bereaved parents will too.

Last week I was told that my continued involvement with TCF was definitely unhealthy. My daughter had been dead for ten years – ten years! – and it was all very sad but, really, one shouldn't dwell on such events. Long-time contact with other people in my situation is "indulging" in death and grief, and that's wrong. Well, isn't it?

My friend is not the first to make this type of comment. Yet, if I were a paid co-ordinator of a TCF centre or, better still, set up in practice as a bereavement counsellor and charging accordingly, there would be smiling approval – I'd be doing something useful with my life...

Actually, I don't provide direct support to grieving parents. My TCF work is in different areas altogether but I deeply resent being told that it's time I stopped anyway. Who would criticise people staying involved in a sporting club when they can no longer take part themselves? Is it an indulgence to volunteer for the Meals on Wheels service and being confronted with the ravages of old age? What about hospice volunteers, are they unhealthy because they work for and with the dying?

It took a long time before I realised what causes so much disapproval. It's not because most of us don't get paid. It's because we are tainted by a great taboo and we refuse to pretend our child's death can be ignored. Not only do we talk about our dead children, we also get emotional, alone and with each other. That's very frightening to many people. If only they could get us away from "that" group, we wouldn't be thinking about that child so much and life with us would be back to normal. In other words, we would no longer act as a reminder of the horrifying possibility that one of their own children could die.

Our volunteer work is further devalued because it is seen as fulfilling an emotional need in ourselves. Certainly there is some truth in the assumption that we help others because of our own inner need. There is also a risk that we become dependent on the feeling of having others rely on us instead of helping them to become strong again themselves. Are bereaved parents any different in this respect from other volunteers? We all hope that our compassion doesn't turn into our compulsion and if that does happen we'll be able to take remedial action.

In the meantime, we can do without the condemnation. Compassion is in short supply in the world. This is one way we have chosen to honour the lives of our dead children; leave us to get on with it.

Eva Lager. TCF Perth, Western Australia

Never apologise for showing feeling. When you do so, you apologise for the truth.

Benjamin Disraeli

Let's be honest...
Why can't I be honest,
when you ask me how I am?
Why do I feel I must pretend
that everything is fine?
Why can't I tell you,
I'm not coping well at all,
that underneath this façade
my heart is broken in two?

Are you afraid I might break down,
if you mention my son's name?
It's almost as if by saying "Will"
you will remind me of him.
Don't you know all I want to do,
is talk about him, all the time?

Are you concerned you might not cope,
if I share my pain with you?
Are you afraid if I start to weep,
you might start crying too?
Or is it because it is easier,
if I pretend I'm OK?
Then you can choose to believe me,
it's easier for you that way.

If you really want to help,
walk with me, and share my grief,
be prepared to hold my hand,
weep with me when I weep.
Listen, when I express my agony,
suffer with me, feel my pain.

If you can do that for me
you are a friend indeed.

Gill Hartley

Faceless
I am standing behind
a two-way mirror,
I see others
but they don't see me.

I have been quite lonely,
it's a pleasure
seeing someone I know.
I smile in expectation
then realise...
they are not seeing me.

Gill Hartley

Whilst waiting to see my GP one morning, a man walked into the waiting room whom I recognised but had not seen for a few years. He used to come to one of the art groups I ran in our village. We talked, catching up with one another's news and I told him about Will. It transpired then that he, too, had lost a child, his ten-year old son, thirty years ago. He then said the words I have heard so often since Will died, "No one understands, do they?" It is this feeling of being misunderstood that unites bereaved parents and the reason why organisations such as TCF exist and are so valuable. Sadly, this man did not know about TCF, although it had already been in existence for ten years when his son died.

> 'Time does not heal,
> It makes a half-stitched scar
> That can be broken and you feel
> Grief as total as in its first hour.'
>
> **Elizabeth Jennings**

Fences

> I was broken, defeated,
> starved for friendship, for care.
> I peered out from the shadows,
> and you were not there.
>
> How would it have hurt you?
> Was it too dark to see?
> What would you have lost
> by befriending me?
>
> I'm surviving and learning,
> have found friendships true.
> And how about you, old friend?
> How is it with you?
>
> **Genesse Gentry**

One morning, three years since Will died and shortly after what would have been his twenty-sixth birthday, I got up early after a particularly sleepless and tearful night, went into his room, turned on the computer and wrote about my feelings. I did not write it with the intention of sending it to the quarterly TCF journal but decided to do so in the hope others might identify with my feelings. I am including the article here:

How do I feel? How do I really feel? No one wants to know how I really feel. What would they say if I told them the truth? That part of me has died, shrivelled up inside me and I have a dried up sponge where my heart used to be. I have a constant dull ache in my stomach, I often feel on the verge of tears but the tears do not fall easily. I have become so used to holding them back so as not to embarrass others, that I find, even when I am on my own, I hold the tears in check. I am my own worst critic now, so fearful that people will think me weak that I judge myself too. I have to be strong, or at least be seen to be strong. Then are the feelings of isolation, that I am not good company and people seek to avoid me. It is easier to avoid me than to take the risk that I might mention Will's name, that I might want to talk about him. After all it is now three years since Will died. I should be getting on with my life, finding new interests.

I feel especially isolated from the church. I haven't attended church services since Will died, except for the very early days when I did attempt to go with my husband. But I found it so difficult. I inevitably wept when any worship songs that I especially associated with Will were played, found it unbearable and had to leave, conscious of the curious looks from members of the church who did not know about Will. I could not go on like this week after week, what would people think? I felt uncomfortable displaying my grief in front of everyone. And there was the added trauma of the memory of Will's coffin on the altar steps and the fact that the two seats where Will and I used to sit often seemed to be unoccupied.

I still feel I want to go into the church when a service is in progress. Go to the front of the church and shout at everyone, "Why don't you understand? How can you possibly think that I can ever get over losing my son? How would you feel if you had your entire family taken away from you? For those of you with more than one child, it would be like losing all your children and grandchildren. It would be like losing your extended family and your future with them. Can you really imagine what that would be like? How would you feel if you had to stand by your child's bed and watch him suffer and die? The child you had cherished and loved more than life itself? Can you imagine how it feels to wake every morning and know that you are never going to see your child again? Never hold him in your arms, hear his voice, tell him you love him? You can't imagine because you don't want to. It doesn't bear thinking about and it is dangerous to get too close to me in case the same thing happens to you. It might be catching. It is much easier to stand in your pulpits and judge me. Judge me for my lack of faith. As a Christian I should not be feeling like this, after all my son is in a "better place" and lost in "Glory and Wonder". I pray that is true but what about me, his mother? How am I expected to find that a comfort when my son is no longer part of my life here? Can't you understand that it is not about faith? It is about grief. Raw, unspeakable, unendurable, agonising grief. In a nutshell, I miss him. I long for him. I don't want to go on living without him. But I am. I am still here after three years without him. Isn't that an achievement in itself? Isn't it enough that I get up and dress in the morning? Isn't it enough that I am trying to live as normal a life as possible with the constant knowledge that life will never be normal again? I don't want to be told that I will find joy again. And happiness.

Is it really so hard to understand that I can never, ever again be truly happy? I will only experience joy when I am reunited with my son, wherever and whenever that might be."

I do try to take an interest in the lives of others. But it is not easy. I am so aware that their lives have moved on and I understand that. I only wish I could explain that it is not always easy for me to listen when they talk about their children and grandchildren. I berate myself for feeling envious at times but is it really so surprising? How can I not feel a little envious when I listen to women talk about such occasions as Mothering Sunday and how wonderful their sons or daughters were to them? I long sometimes to join in the conversation, if only to say how thoughtful Will was and how he always bought me beautiful white flowers on Mothering Sunday and made me special cards, how he used to write on the backs of the cards, "That Special Moment. Hartley Cards. Est. 1983" (Will's birth date). I would love to tell them but I know if I do it will only cause an awkward silence and a change of subject. I cannot pretend Will never existed and have heard so many parents say the same of their children. Our children were, and still are, a precious part of our lives and we should have the right to talk freely about them, not feel that we must keep quiet in order to make others feel more comfortable.

Isn't it time that as a nation we learned to cope with grief? Death is part of living. One thing we can be certain of in life is that each of us will die sooner or later. It is often said that we begin to die from the moment we are born and that is true. We are all destined to live here on earth for our allotted span and then die. So why is death such a taboo subject? Why are we embarrassed by grief and feel we must be strong and wear the very British "stiff upper lip?" I have lost count of the number of times people have said to me that I am "looking better" and "doing very well". Firstly, I have not been ill; bereavement is a fact of life, and not an illness and I will never "be better". I will continue to grieve for my son until the day I die. I still lie awake longing for him and weep myself to sleep. And, secondly, I am not "doing very well". I am simply surviving and, sadly, having to learn to live with the absence of my dearest son. I will never recover from his death but I am finding ways to cope and to ward off the insensitivity of others. I often say, "Pass" if someone thinks to ask how I am. I don't want to be dishonest. At the same time I don't want to embarrass them or make them wish they hadn't asked by telling them the truth. We British have a bad habit of asking how someone is without really wanting to know or hear the answer. And we have all learned to answer, "I'm fine thank you. How are you?"

I hope all this does not make me sound bitter. I try hard not to be but there are times when the unfairness of it all overwhelms me and yet I know that life is unfair and none of us can expect to be singled out to live a charmed existence.

My son was a wonderful young man. He looked like an angel with his beautiful silver blond hair and hazel eyes. He was kind, caring, compassionate, funny, clever and exceptionally thoughtful. He even kept the dates of his friends' birthdays in his diary and kept record of the birthday dates of the children in my family. He had a genuine concern for others and wisdom beyond his years. He was the light of my life. I adored him and he, in turn, adored me. We were unusually close; he was my soul mate, my closest friend. Not only have I lost my baby, the baby I carried for nine months. I have also lost the child I suckled, nurtured, educated, and encouraged, the beautiful child who accompanied me everywhere before he started school. I have lost the bright happy schoolboy I ferried to and from school every day. I have lost the boy who became a teenager and went on to study at university. The handsome young man who wanted to give his life to God and become an Anglican minister. The friend who phoned me every day, with whom I talked for hours and listened as he shared his hopes and dreams. The young man who could always make me laugh with his dry and quirky sense of humour.

I have lost all this and much, much more. I cannot simply put a stop to all this and "move on" with my life. It is too easy for others to say, "Well, at least you had him for twenty-two years." Would they like to put a limit on the number of years that their children will live for? How can the fact that our children lived for one, five, ten, twenty or forty years and died before us be of any consolation? It is the wrong order of things; we are not supposed to bury our children.

Our children are our future, we want to see them marry, hold our grandchildren in our arms and smile at the family likeness. A little bit of ourselves carrying on into the future. Will was unmarried and our only child and like many parents in our position, we will never be grandparents. And so we are told, "Well, he might not have got married." Or "He might not have had children." Oh well, that's all right then. But all I know is that Will dearly wanted to marry and have children and I have every reason to believe he would. If it had turned out that he and his wife could not have children, then we would have faced that disappointment with him. It is quite a different matter to know that it will never, ever happen. Not now. Not ever.

All I do know is that Will doesn't phone me every day the way he used to. I can't hear his voice or hear him laugh. I can't hold him or touch him. I can't tell him how much I love him and hear his voice saying, "I love you, Mum."

There are times when I feel suicidal. I know that I have to be here but I don't want to be. I know that I should be thankful that I am alive and count the blessings I have. I know that I have to be

77

here for Edwin, that I cannot leave him alone. But I am frightened. I am frightened of the future. I am frightened of being alone. Sadly, like many other bereaved parents, we are not surrounded by supportive family and friends. Our respective families could not cope with Will's death and we seldom hear from them. Old friends simply disappeared. Outside of TCF, I do have a few good friends who are there for me. But there are times when even they confess that they do not really understand the depth of my pain and, to be fair, how can they?

I do not know what to do to change the way I feel. I feel put down, misunderstood, and terribly, terribly, lonely. I feel so insecure. I feel that the more time passes, the harder and more of a battle it becomes just to survive. It is as if Will never existed, except in my imagination. But he did exist and that is why I have to hold on tightly to all that proves his existence. He lived for nearly 23 years and was a gift to everyone he met. But the fact that there is hardly anyone with whom I can share memories of him is literally sapping all the life force out of me. It is slowly strangling me. Draining me of all the interests I once held dear and which kept me on my feet. Even tending to the garden seems pointless now.

Like all of us, I do try. I have written a collection of poetry as a tribute to Will, which was published last year. I am giving talks on the subject of losing a child, in the hopes of raising awareness and suggesting ways others can help bereaved parents and come alongside them. I am surviving. And that is all I can do.

Many parents wrote to me following the publication of this article in Compassion, expressing their own disappointment at the lack of understanding they felt they had encountered at their own church. I have read many books on the Christian attitude to death and the belief in a life to come. I share that belief and hold on to it but it does not take away the pain of living on here without my son...

The following words by CS Lewis reflect similar sentiments. I found it so difficult when well meaning friends quoted scripture to me and in his book, "A Grief Observed", Lewis says, *"Talk to me about the truth of religion and I'll listen gladly. Talk to me about the duty and I'll listen submissively. But don't come talking to me about the consolations of religion or I shall suspect you don't understand."*

Unfortunately, this belief can get in the way of a realistic understanding of the pain of bereavement. In his excellent book, God of the Valley, the Rev. Steve Griffiths discusses this problem. Steve wrote his book following the death of his young wife, his sister and a close friend. He was expected to continue with his duties as a minister without help or a true understanding of his grief. He writes,

> *"For many of us there is that unspoken expectation for us to worship God and play a full part in the life of the church throughout our time of grief."*

He also believes that, *"It is extremely harmful for us to cover up anger and hurt beneath a façade of happiness."*

Following on from the beatitude *"Blessed are those who mourn, for they shall be comforted"* Steve also says,

> *"This is the mandate of God for those who hurt. Sadly, however, it is not always the experience of those who turn to the church for solace. Too often, those who are recently bereaved or divorced are the subjects of unspoken judgement".* He goes on to say, *"Sometimes the deprivation of comfort is less harsh than that but just as damaging. This is particularly the case with the bereaved, who may be well supported in the initial stages of grief but, after six months or so, find themselves passed over for the next 'needy case' that has come along. By the time we have to face our first Christmas alone, our first birthday alone, the Christian community seems to have moved on. We are left alone and comfortless – and it hurts."*

I felt that I was somehow "letting the side down" by being unable to attend church and worship the God by whom I felt betrayed, particularly when our church had been so supportive throughout Will's illness.

Although others did seek to comfort me, I felt uncomfortable at displaying my grief in front of everyone, week after week; after all, it is not very "British" is it? And being told that Will was in a better place and "lost in glory and wonder" did not help at all. I wanted him here, with me. Such comments only served to make me feel selfish and misunderstood.

I wish now that I had been able to weep more openly. My attempts to swallow my tears were not helpful to me and, if anything, seemed to alienate others because these feelings led me to withdraw and, sadly, people did not understand this and thought I preferred to be left alone.

"One of us fell off the boat. Look in our faces, read our eyes as we come ashore. One of us fell off the boat. We're back. In our homes, you can see that there are times when we hate surviving. There are times when we think how easy to have been him. One wave and gone."

Michael Rosen

Solitude
LAUGH and the world laughs with you;
Weep and you weep alone,
For the sad old world must borrow its mirth
But has trouble enough of its own.

Ella Wheeler Wilcox

A friend from our church very kindly helped me with my website, as although I have had to acquire some computer skills now that Will is no longer here to help me, designing and creating websites is certainly not one of them!

This friend made the following comments after reading through some of the articles she had put onto my web page for me and I think that her observations are worth including in this book.

I, doubtless along with many others, hate to see your pain. I don't think there is a lack of care or fear of contagion here. There is, however, an expectation that the church can alleviate suffering; when this is not the case, it delivers a profound sense of helplessness. It is easy to think that the suffering person is somehow 'not trying'. Awkwardness and embarrassment set in and eventually lead to isolation.

We all like to think that our friends will support us through thick and thin. I think this is unreasonable - friendships are built on shared experiences and passions. You are not the person you were, and it is natural that your friends should now be different.

A very long time ago, I listened to a sermon at a missionary valedictory service. I remember it because it fitted my circumstances at the time, and it has come back to me now. The bottom line was 'Trust God, not man'.

This, of course was written from a Christian viewpoint and I realise that not everyone who reads this will have a faith in God. I can so understand, as it is hard to see, especially when we lose a cherished child, how a loving God could "allow" this to happen. We will never know the answers to the burning question, "Why?" but I try to hold on to my Christian faith and the belief that, one day, it will all make sense.

The friends who in our sunshine live,
When winter comes, are flown;
And he who has but tears to give,
Must weep those tears alone.
But Thou wilt heal that broken heart,
Which, like the plants that throw
Their fragrance from the wounded part,
Breathes sweetness out of woe.

Thomas Moore

"For such as he there is no death;
His life the eternal life commands;
O lonely friend! He still will be
A potent presence, though unseen,
Steadfast, sagacious, and serene;
Seek not for him - he is with thee."
Louisa May Alcott

A friend who is far away is sometimes much nearer than one
who is at hand. Is not the mountain far more awe-inspiring
and more clearly visible to one passing through the valley than
to those who inhabit the mountain?
Khalil Gibran

Two people are better off than one, for they can help each other
succeed. If one person falls, the other can reach out and help.
But someone who falls alone is in real trouble. Likewise, two
people lying close together can keep each other warm. But how
can one be warm alone? A person standing alone can be
attacked and defeated, but two can stand back-to-back and
conquer. Three are even better, for a triple-braided cord is not
easily broken.
Ecclesiastes 4:9–12.

Sometimes it is hard to try and understand when others are unable to support us. We tell ourselves that they don't know what to say, that they do not understand the depth of our loss. Sadly this has a ring of truth, as I don't think I would really have understood the agony of losing a child before Will died. I say this despite having lived next door to the neighbours who lost their only child and subsequently carried the fear of having and losing an only child throughout my life – it is only now that I look back and realise exactly the pain our neighbours endured and how generous they were to be so good to us. The first time I wrote to the TCF journal, Compassion, I included a couple of poems I had written about the things people say to us – the unthinking comments, the clichés. I will always remember the editor's response. "It seems," she said, "that when we are most in need of tolerance and understanding, we have to find it in ourselves for others." How true those words are. The following extract from Auden's poem, "As I Walked Out One Evening" echoes those sentiments so well.

'O stand, stand at the window
As the tears scald and start;
You shall love your crooked neighbour
With your crooked heart.'

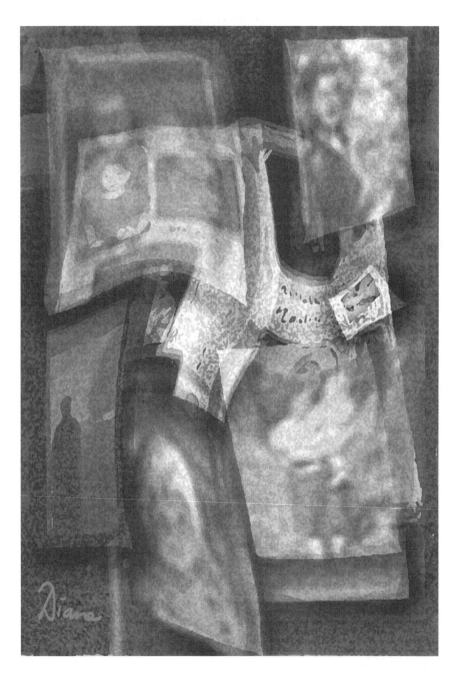

Albums

Autumn's golden coins
Drift from trees with memories
Treading leaves with you

Our memories of our children's lives and the precious moments spent with them are stored in our minds like photographs in an album. When we see or think of something which takes us back to a certain time, we select a page from that album of memories and bring it to life.

For Will's beautiful funeral service, we created a collage of photos of him; from his very first photo to the most recent and displayed them on the large notice board in the church hall, where the reception would be held after the service. When we rummaged through all the photographs for the reception, we were still in that unreal world we find ourselves in after our child dies and I was able to look through the pictures and select the ones I wanted to display. But when I wanted to recreate the collage for our kitchen wall, I found that looking at photographs of Will caused me so much pain that I could not look at them. I managed to cope with the framed photographs around the house that we had not taken to the church. But when anyone gave me a photo of Will I had not seen before, or I saw a photo of Will I had not looked at for a while, it felled me and I could not cope with it.

When I worked on my first book, a collection of poetry for Will, I wanted to use photographs as illustrations. This meant I had to look through the numerous albums and boxes of photographs and, gradually, I began to deal with the pain and find comfort in them. I still struggle at times and when I look at Will's beautiful face, smiling gently at me from a picture frame, it fills me with such longing that sometimes I have to look away.

We recently bought one of those large clipboard frames and at last I found the courage to look and sort through all the photographs of Will. It took me two days to assemble some of the photographs on the clipboard; two tearful and heart-rending days. But I managed to do it and we now have the collage on our kitchen wall.

A few days after we had put the collage up, some friends from TCF came to spend the weekend with us. It was a joy to share the pictures with them and a special joy to be able to talk about Will and the memories the photographs invoked. I am so thankful now that I at last found the courage to recreate the collage and our friends left after the weekend, saying they wanted to go home and create collages of their sons. Since then other non-TCF friends have shared looking at the photographs and this has helped us. For parents in a similar situation to ours, with families who have not coped with the grief and kept their distance, to be able to share such visual memories has been very valuable, even with those who did not know Will during his lifetime.

Because we had to move our kitchen clock to another place to make room for the collage, every time I checked the time I found myself looking at Will instead. But now I am beginning to find that the pictures are bringing me comfort and an increased closeness to Will. I am now preparing a second collage, this time including pictures of the children of some of our TCF friends. Of course the photographs still fill me with longing. But I am so thankful that I have been able to do this and do not live in an age when photographs did not exist or in a third world country where this would not have been an option.

The Photograph

*At first I almost took the photograph
down. It showed the two of us
together, walking in the Chiltern hills.*

*We stopped for a rest. I leant
against you, your arm round me,
my head on your shoulder.*

*The pain I felt each time I saw it
was so acute, it made me feel
again my overwhelming loss.*

*But to stare at the space it would
leave would be worse. So it
stayed. And gradually as*

time passed, I made a friend of pain.
And now, in moments of anxiety,
I stand and look at the photograph.

I lean on you still and will all
my life. Your arm around me.
My head on your shoulder.

Gina Claye

In memory's telephoto lens, far objects are magnified.
John Updike

Sue White's young son, Paul, died in a car accident at the age of eighteen. Sue has written many moving poems for her son, some of which are included in this book. I think this poem of Sue's expresses so well our feelings when we look at photographs of our children...

The Artist's Gift
A moment of peace when time stood still
Now eternity whispers your name
A flickering candle casts a shadow
Upon a timeless smile captured in a frame
Trailing fingers ache to touch soft strands of hair
But trapped behind an unyielding prison
You exist but are not there
Eyes alight with laughter straining to escape
A lifetime of memories locked in silence
Watchful of every move I make
Soft and warm your face pressed against the icy glass
The blush of youth immortalised by painter's hand
Gives lie to beating heart
Breathe in, breathe out, no sound at all
Child of my heart
Stilled, silenced
A picture on a wall

Sue White

Sue also wrote the following article, "Frozen in Time"

I know how lucky I am to have so many photographs of Paul, moments where we captured the laughter, the fun and that beautiful smile people have always remembered. There are just a few images of a pensive Paul caught up in a world of his own dreams, maybe of his future or mischief making! Then there is just one photograph taken of a little boy where he couldn't get his own way and his face screwed up in frustration is immortalised.

In the early stages of my grief, the photographs would tip me into a world of pain and yet we had them everywhere. Every room held those frozen images, so that I was never without him. No matter which way I turned, my beautiful son was smiling at me.

Shock in those early days and months meant I never really saw those photographs for what they were. He was there and yet he was not there. Maybe subconsciously we had put them there so that other people on their visits would know he was our son and always would be and we did not want him banished to the past..

Shock kept me in its control until the advent of the first anniversary, when the photographs began to provoke agonising pain. I would look at those images of Paul and want to smash the glass, so that I could free him and hold him again.

He had been frozen in time, immortalised in the past, accessible only under glass where fingers that ached to touch him were frustrated by a solid barrier, and eyes that longed to watch him move saw nothing; no breath rippled the surface of the photograph.

I have found it incredibly difficult each year to adjust to watching the age gap between Gary and Paul stretch with each year and, sadly, with each new photograph of Gary as he ages and enjoys each stage of his life, is the pain of knowing that Paul has become a child who does not age. It is unnatural. A forever kind of suffering for those of us left behind.

Some other poems evoke the feelings we have when we look at those photographs…

WHEN we were parted, sweet, and darkness came,
I used to strike a match, and hold the flame
Before your picture and would breathless mark
The answering glimmer of the tiny spark
That brought to life the magic of your eyes,
Their wistful tenderness, their glad surprise.
Holding that mimic torch before your shrine
I used to light your eyes and make them mine;
Watch them like stars set in a lonely sky,
Whisper my heart out, yearning for reply;
Summon your lips from far across the sea
Bidding them live a twilight hour with me.
Then, when the match was shrivelled into gloom,
Lo--you were with me in the darkened room.
Christopher Morley

The Long Wood
Looking back up the stream, up the years,
I still see your face smiling sun-caught
In the leaf-filtered bright between high banks.
And running splashes ever echo as your smile
Ripples outward into time and your laugh
Sings on, as you look suddenly
Down the stream at me.

My heart aches at your instant of happiness
But not so much as it does now,
These short years gone.
Barrie Shaw

When I first moved away
From the home where he toddled
And grew to manhood,
I was afraid of leaving memories
Too precious to lose forever.

That house held all his life,
In its walls were the echoes of his music,
The garden full of his flowers.
I gathered together possessions,
Books, clothes, guitar and photographs,
Yes, especially the photographs,
Marking his progress through life:
The smiling chubby baby,
The school boy with his friends,
The young man, windblown on top of a mountain;
Then brimful of success in cap and gown.
And, standing straight and tall
With his bride, happy on his wedding day.

All these I took with me for solace,
In new surroundings which might
Prove to be overwhelming.

I need not have worried
His love and his presence came with me,
His face is in every room,
His smiles uplift me every day.

Eileen Whatmough TCF mother

We cannot judge a biography by its length, by the number of
pages in it; we must judge by the richness of its contents....
Sometimes the 'unfinished' are among the most beautiful
symphonies.

Victor Frankl

I first met Charles Coulson at the 40th anniversary gathering of The Compassionate Friends. He has kindly given his permission for me to include the two poems below, written following the unexplained suicide of his eighteen year old son, James, an art student. Charles writes,

"Desktop Photos" reflects a life lived for a short time with my father, and a life lived for a short time with my son. I was a child of eight when my father died at home as a result of prostate cancer. I was shielded from both his death and the funeral because, "I might have been upset." Distance shielded me from the tragic death of my son and only child. A photograph of my father, unearthed from a box of family archives was framed by my wife. My father's and his grandson's photos stand together on my desk. A sudden realisation they had never met in this life was the inspiration for the poem.

On my desktop
Two photos
Father and son
Father, dead
I was just a boy
Son, dead
He was just a man
On a near shore
Father and son
Await
Son and father

Charles Coulson

"The Unfinished Portrait" was inspired and written at Gill's poetry workshop at the Compassionate Friends 40th Anniversary Gathering. The portrait of Jim's girlfriend Nicky was unfinished for reasons unknown. It hangs at the top of the stairs and as the poem states it reflects a life unfinished. I would add the poem was written in a very short time and is a first and final draft.

Unfinished portrait
Brushed with oils of red and blue
Your life incomplete.

Charles Coulson

91

Photographs are precious in helping us to remember our child, as the following poem captures so well. I can remember being frightened I would forget what Will looked and sounded like – a fear shared by many parents, especially in the early days of our grief. I have found, as time passes, the fear has receded a little, although there are still times when I wonder if Will was ever really here at all. But I know that he was and although the photos are very precious, he lives on in my heart and soul and is now a part of who I am.

That look on your face says it all,
"Oh, mum, not the camera again!"
You made fun of me taking photos
At every opportunity.
At family parties, six or seven cameras
Taking the same shot.
"What's the point?" You'd say.
But what would I do without
Those photos now?
I could not look at them and
Remember the occasion – go back...
The time, the place, why we were there,
What we ate, what we did.
I can touch the photos and almost
Feel your skin, the fabric of your clothes, your hair.
I can hear your voice.
These photos bring you back to me.

Julie Donnelly,
TCF mother

YOU walked beside me, quick and free;
With lingering touch you grasped my hand;
Your eyes looked laughingly in mine;
And now ? I can not understand.
I long for you, I mourn for you,
Through all the dark and lonely hours.

Sarah Orne Jewett

We bought Will a camera for his twenty-first birthday and he soon became a very keen and knowledgeable photographer. He had always taken photos but not with what he called "a real camera". Now the walls of his room are adorned with photographs he took and I have a heap of the photo magazines he bought regularly – I cannot part with them. Like everything that Will took an interest in, he researched and invested much time and enthusiasm.

I wrote the following poem in memory of my mother but I am including it here, as I think it captures the thought that we keep our memories in albums in our minds.

Roses
This spring I cut the roses back hard,
tried to cut out all the dead wood.
You taught me how to prune a rose,
find a bud and cut just above it,
at a slant, so the flower grows free.
Now you are no longer with me,
my memories entwine with your scent.
Petals pressed between mellowing leaves,
Sweet Briar, your thorns still embrace me.

This summer I will pick the roses,
just the way you did,
full blown and heavy with dew.

Gill Hartley

When our child dies, people like to tell us that we have our memories. Yes, we do have our memories but, for some time, we find the memories hurt. Remembering fills us with longing and grief for all we have lost. There will come a time when the memories become less painful but they will always be bitter sweet.

Bright shards of sunshine
Pierced the sunlit air,
As you ran, laughing,
Back to me,
Breathless
From wrestling with the boisterous sea
To join me on the sand,
The sparkling droplets from your hair,
As I reached up to touch you,
A shower of sparkling diamonds
Splintering
Against my sun-warmed hand.

And, as I saw you grin,
  (my first reaction
  to those tiny icicles
  of chill against my skin
  more instinct than surprise!)
The surge of answering laughter bubbling up inside
Caught in my throat...
And suddenly I was breathless, too,
Breathless with love for you,
A love that I saw mirrored in your eyes.

Bright shards of happiness remembered:
Oh, how they pierce my heart,
Remembering.

Gloria Burles

Kathy Duggan's brother died in 1964 at the age of seventeen. I think her words capture the feeling that the world as we knew it has come to a halt, everything has turned upside down...

Somersault

This is the summer you went away.
This is the rosehip that twined
through the beech
in the summer you went away.
This is the bird that burst
through the beech round which the rose twined
in the summer you went away.
This is the butterfly
painting the lane that was
baked by the sun
by which the beech grew
through which the rose twined
from where the bird flew
in the summer you went away.
And these are the seeds that crackle and fly
at the touch of my hand
in the silent July.
Here grow the nettles
beside the combed corn
among the warm thistledown
soft as your hair
on the day you were born.
And this is the sun
that shines in the night
and this is the moon
that shines in the day
and this is the somersault
made by the world
the summer you went away.

Kathy Duggan

But memory is the only friend
That grief can call its own.

Alfred Bunn

Speech is silver

The proverb speaks of silence being golden
and speech as silver, like your precious voice,
living in my memory like an echo
a silver sword plunged deep into my heart.
I cannot bear the silence of your leaving
memories of you drift like gentle rain,
I want to capture every golden moment -
use silver threads to sew them in my soul.

Gill Hartley

It stunned me when a friend expressed surprise that Mothering Sunday was a painful day for me. I don't know why she was surprised. Maybe because as we grow older, we are more likely to have lost our mothers and that was in her mind or whether because we associate Mothering Sunday with small children presenting their mothers with hand made cards and presents. Actually, for many bereaved mothers it is one of the most poignant days of the year. Even more so when the child was the only child. We feel we have lost our role, that we are no longer mothers. We are, of course, but not in the sense that our precious child is here with us. C S Lewis wrote,

> *"If a mother is mourning not for what she has lost but for what her dead child has lost, it is a comfort to believe that the child has not lost the end for which it was created. A comfort to the God-aimed, eternal spirit within her. But not to her motherhood. The specifically maternal happiness must be written off. Never, in any place or time, will she have her son on her knees, or bathe him or tell him a story, or plan for his future, or see her grandchild."*

Rain, relentless rain.
So many people,
So many bringing flowers
To honour their mothers.
Those more fortunate mothers –
Who died first.
The right way round.

Diane Shepherd

Mothering Sunday

I am sitting here,
holding the beautiful card
you made for me, ...

two years ago, today.

I have twenty-one such cards from you,
and treasure every one.
From the first card,
bought by your father,
and scribbled on, by you.
to the card I am holding now.

As my tears fall,
I reflect,
maybe we have got it wrong
as mothers we should give our children the cards,
for teaching us the meaning
of love.

My darling Will,
I'll try to dry my tears,
and dedicate this special day,
my precious son...

to you.   **Gill Hartley**
                                 From: My True Son, 2008

Cemetery

Sitting here with one you love
Shouldn't be difficult you might think?
Except that my someone –
My particular someone –
Died some years ago.

He didn't like the cold.
My son didn't like the cold,
And here I sit,
In the cold,
Remembering him warm.

                              Diane Shepherd

Last Night

The end was near
and so I spent the night beside you in the chair,
for fear that you would leave me softly in the darkness
while I slept on
or wake from that deep well you lay in,
one final time,
and I not be there
to glimpse a last connection in your eyes.

You did not waken,
though at times your eyes would open and I'd speak your name,
but you were gone from me already.
And, some time in the darkest, stillest hours,
I took your hand and held it, warm, against my breast.
All that night long I held it there,
your skin and mine as they belonged,
together,
till morning came.

Jill White

Futility

She searches everywhere, hoping to find it,
rummages in untidy cupboards and drawers,
looks under the bed, behind the curtains,
moves paper piles from one place to another,
turns out the files, upsets the waste bin.
It's nowhere it seems but must be somewhere.

She searches now in sheer desperation
longing to find what she knows she has lost,
yet all the time knowing her search is futile,
how can she recover her life as it was...

Gill Hartley

I love the following poem. Although it was not written about the death of a child, I think it captures beautifully the emotions we feel when we think of those we have loved and the memories of precious moments in time.

Something of the child...

Your father loved to paddle.
In an old photo I have seen him
Trousers rolled, ankle deep
In the shallows at Southend
A big grin on his face.
The photographer has caught
An act of rebellion,
A stance against convention, expectation,
Daily frustration at the Bank,
Something of the child in the man.

Now on this wide open beach,
Empty of people,
Full of seabirds, sands shifting in the wind
Conditions are pronounced, "just right".
You have been threatening this for ages
So I have brought a towel.
These days your balance is not so good.
You lean against me lightly taking off your shoes,
Walk carefully into
The shallow, even waves.

I keep pace on the sand as you walk
(Though I know you want to run).
"Oh, come on, it is so fresh, feels so good."
No, I am sensible and shorebound, taking pictures,
Holding the towel.
But watching your pleasure
The wind is getting into my eyes
Making them water.

Rachel Irven

Of the deepest share of pain;
Here the deepest bliss to treasure
Memories of that cry of pleasure;
Hers to hoard, a lifetime after,
Echoes of that infant laughter.

Laman Lanchart:
From "The Mother's Hope"

I have selected the following poems because I believe they reflect our ongoing sadness, a sadness that will always be a part of our lives.

Memories
Tender, fragile
Shared, beautiful, strong
Never, ever, forgotten
Thoughts

Edwin Hartley

You are the rarest soul I ever knew,
Lover of beauty, knightliest and best,
My thoughts seek you as waves that seek the shore,
And when I think of you I am at rest.

Sara Teasdale

Only, from the long line of spray
Where the sea meets the moon-blanched land,
Listen! you hear the grating roar
Of pebbles which the waves draw back, and fling
At their return, up the high strand,
Begin, and cease, and then again, begin
With tremulous cadence slow, and bring
The eternal note of sadness in.

Matthew Arnold
From "Forsaken Merman"

The leaves of memory seemed to make
A mournful rustling in the dark.

Henry Wadsworth Longfellow

So lie the wasted gifts, the long-lost hopes,
Beneath the now hushed surface of myself,
In lonelier depths than where the diver gropes;
They lie deep, deep; but I at times behold
In doubtful glimpses, on some reefy shelf,
The gleam of irrecoverable gold.

Eugene Lee-Hamilton

He Wishes for the Cloths of Heaven

Had I the heavens' embroidered cloths,
Enwrought with golden and silver light,
The blue and the dim and the dark cloths
Of night and light and the half-light,
I would spread the cloths under your feet:
But I, being poor, have only my dreams;
I have spread my dreams under your feet;
Tread softly because you tread on my dreams.

W.B Yeats

I close the book;
But the past slides out of its leaves to haunt me
And it seems, wherever I look,
Phantoms of irreclaimable happiness taunt me.

C Day-Lewis

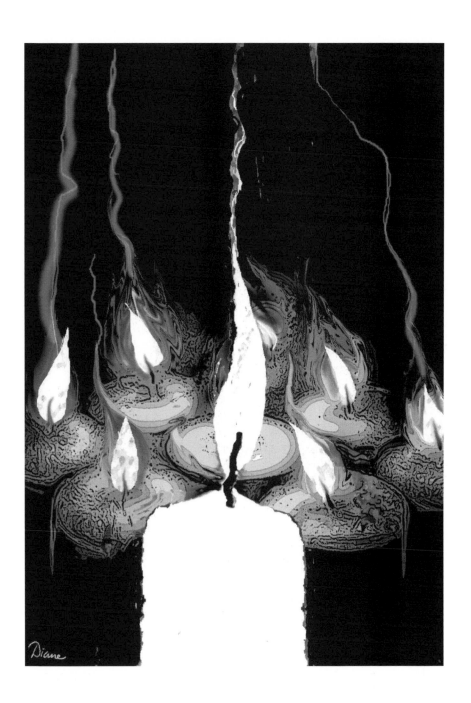

Diane

102

Candles

Candles
Glowing, shining.
Flickering flame brings hope
And light into our darkest hours
Son Light

Gill Hartley

Many bereaved people find much solace in lighting candles in memory of their loved ones. There is something very comforting in watching the flickering flame and thinking of how the candlelight penetrates the darkness. It is somehow symbolic of the eternal flame and connects us to the hope of eternal life and the joy of seeing our loved ones again. In some of the older churches and cathedrals you can light candles and many churches hold annual remembrance services and members of the congregation are invited to light a candle in remembrance of their loved ones. Whenever I visit a church that has candles, I always light a row of them if possible - one for Will and for all the other lost children. And pray for Will and for them.

The Compassionate Friends hold a worldwide candle lighting day before Christmas every year and bereaved parents around the world light a candle at 7pm local time. It is very moving when we do that and we can almost feel the presence of the thousands of bereaved parents and their children and know we are not alone

In October 2009, my husband and I attended the fortieth anniversary gathering of The Compassionate Friends. This was a residential weekend held at Bosworth Hall in Warwickshire and the first national gathering we had been to. It was quite an experience to be with so many bereaved parents from all over the country and abroad.

The most poignant moment for most of us must have been the display of the names of all of our children after dinner on Friday evening. A candle in a safety cup was placed on each parent's table setting and a lit candle in the centre of each table. On a sky blue screen, to the accompaniment of some very moving TCF songs, our children's names appeared, one by one in alphabetical order, moving up the screen to disappear before the next name appeared. We were asked to light our individual candle when our child's name was shown. It was almost unbearable to watch as parent after parent leaned forward to light his or her candle until every table in the room was adorned with burning lights. It was an unexpected, touching and very tearful event.

One of the mothers, Mary Hartley (no relation, although we are now friends) came to the poetry workshop I held at the gathering, desperate to write a poem describing her feelings. I am including the letter Mary sent with her poem, as I think her comments and her very moving poem sum up perfectly the emotions of all the parents who took part in this ceremony.

I found the display of our children's names very emotional and unsettling on Friday night at The Gathering, mostly because I really didn't want my daughter's name to be there. It made her death so definite somehow. On Saturday, I went along to Gill's workshop, determined to get my feelings down on paper...

Names,
Children's names,
I wish yours wasn't there,
But it is.
"Claire"

Mary Hartley

Many poets and writers use the candle to express deep sadness and reflection. The following all capture the essence of the poignancy of candlelight.

And one by one the lamps are lit
In the dome of the Infinite.

From *Nightfall* by
Alexander Lawrence Posey

The Old Woman

As a white candle
In a holy place,
So is the beauty
Of an aged face.

As the spent radiance
Of the winter sun,
So is a woman
With her travail done.

Her brood gone from her,
And her thoughts as still
As the waters
Under a ruined mill.   **Joseph Campbell**

First Fig

My candle burns at both ends
It will not last the night
But oh my foes and oh my friends
It gives a lovely light!
                              Edna St Vincent Millay

Lighting a candle

I lit a candle for you yesterday,
It seemed a comfort as I sat alone
in the sitting room, a joyous presence

as if you'd walked in once again
with your wayward humour and listening heart,
and I sat motionless, held in your love.

Now the candle is cold and I stare
at the unloving wax skin
that once supported the beating flame

and I wonder where you are now.
Are you waiting, stilled and existing
in worlds I know nothing of?

Until that moment
when it is time once again
to light the candle.   **Gina Claye**

In the candlelight
I saw you smiling at me
My heart sang with joy
I wanted to hold you, but
You are frozen in a frame.

Gill Hartley

The words from the following poem by Paul Alexander have been set to music and the resulting song was one of those chosen to accompany the candle lighting ceremony at the 40th anniversary gathering of The Compassionate Friends.

Light a candle
And I will light a candle for you,
To shatter all the darkness and bless the times we knew
Like a beacon in the night
The flame will burn bright and guide us on our way,
Oh, today I light a candle for you.

The seasons come and go, and I'm weary from the change.
I keep moving on, you know it's not the same.
And when I'm walking all alone
Do you hear me call your name?
Do you hear me sing the songs we used to sing?

You filled my world with wonder, touched me with surprise,
Always saw that something special deep within your eyes.
And through the good times and the bad,
We carried on with pride,
I hold on to the love and life we knew.

Paul Alexander
Words and music by Paul Alexander and www.griefsong.com

106

Sometimes our light goes out but it is blown into flame again by an encounter with another human being. Each of us owes the deepest thanks to those who have rekindled this inner light.

Albert Schweitzer

I have an enduring memory of Will, aged two. We were at a friend's son's Christening and Will's voice echoed round the church, "Look. Mummy! Happy Birthday candles."

I rarely dream of Will. Some bereaved parents, especially the mothers, seem to dream regularly of their departed child. The few times I have dreamed of Will are vivid in my memory and I described them in my first collection of poems for him. In the dreams I have always been very aware of the fact that Will has died and the joy of being with him again has been wrought with the pain and sadness of knowing my time with him is only temporary. Yet, that said, when we dream our children are with us again, it can be strangely comforting and bring a little light into our darkness.

The following poem by the American poet, Mark Doty, captures this feeling so movingly.

The Embrace
You weren't well or really ill yet either;
just a little tired, your handsomeness
tinged by grief or anticipation, which brought
to your face a thoughtful, deepening grace.

I didn't for a moment doubt you were dead.
I knew that to be true still, even in the dream.
You'd been out — at work maybe?—
having a good day, almost energetic.

We seemed to be moving from some old house
where we'd lived, boxes everywhere, things
in disarray: that was the story of my dream,
but even asleep I was shocked out of the narrative.

By your face, the physical fact of your face:
inches from mine, smooth-shaven, loving, alert.
Why so difficult, remembering the actual look
of you? Without a photograph, without strain?

So when I saw your unguarded, reliable face,
your unmistakable gaze opening all the warmth
and clarity of you--warm brown tea--we held
each other for the time the dream allowed.

Bless you. You came back, so I could see you
once more, plainly, so I could rest against you
without thinking this happiness lessened anything,
without thinking you were alive again.

Mark Doty

Faith is putting your hand out in the dark and finding it held.

Anon

To dream...
I want to fall asleep and dream of you,
dream that you are here and all is well,
tell you I love you, hold you close,
feel your arms around me, hear your voice
telling me you love me -
I'm the best mum in the world.

I want to wake and find the dream is real,
God has changed His mind and sent you back,
you are once more sleeping in your room.
We laugh together, as we used to do,
I can hear your voice and see your face,
look into your eyes and see you smile,
feel the joy your presence always brought
into my life and brightened up my days.

But, my child, I do not dream of you.
You are not here to brighten every day.
I can only hope that when I die,
I'll dream this dream and wake up in your arms.
When that day comes, the dream will never end
and we will be together evermore.   **Gill Hartley**

Beyond Darkness
When trees, stripped of their ornaments stand,
Black giants lost in dusk and mist, drawn
Like a widow's veil to grieve and mourn,
When birds' songs have ceased and
Their wings no longer beat the air,
When all creatures hide in despair,
When the woods are deserted and I walk alone,
My steps crushing leaves into soil,
I wonder. Have trees always known
Spring will give them back their emeralds?
Does earth know, though wrapped in voile,
Sun will magic life with a sprinkle of gold?
And do we know when our heart has frozen with tears?
      Michelle Gunner

TIPTOEING twilight,
Before you pass,
Bathe light my spirit
As dew bathes grass.
Quiet the longing
Of my hands that yearn,
As you fold the flower
And hush the fern.
Guard me with shadows
To fortify
My failing purpose,
My tired eye,
That in your stillness
I may relight
My faith's frail candle
Before the night.   **Hazel Hall**

Perhaps some day the sun will shine again,
And I shall see that still the skies are blue,
And feel once more I do not live in vain,
Although bereft of You.

Vera Brittain

Watching the flame that carries your name
Gives a sense that you are with me again.
A light that helps me through the blackest night.

I cannot ask the dark to go away
But have to stumble on and wait for day.

Jean Beith, *from her poem: Silent Candle*

I thank Thee, God that I have lived
In this great world and known its many joys;
The song of birds, the strong, sweet scent of hay
And cooling breezes in the secret dusk,
The flaming sunsets at the close of day,
Hills, and the lonely heather-covered moors,
Music at night, and moonlight on the sea,
The beat of waves upon the rocky shore
And wild, white spray, flung high in ecstasy;
The faithful eyes of dogs, and treasured books,
The love of kin, and fellowship of friends,
And all that makes life dear and beautiful.
I thank Thee, too, that there has come to me
A little sorrow, and sometimes defeat,
A little heartache, and the loneliness
That comes with parting, and the word,
"Goodbye",
Dawn breaking after dreary hours of pain,
When I discovered that night's gloom must yield
And morning light break through to me again.
Because of these, and other blessings poured
Unasked upon my wondering head,
Because I know that there is yet to come
An even richer and more glorious life,

And, most of all, because Thine only Son
Once sacrificed life's loveliness for me –
I thank Thee, God, that I have lived.

Elizabeth, Countess of Craven

It was magical
as we walked along the lane
a shaft of sunlight
turned the canopy of leaves
into sparkling golden rain.

Gill Hartley

Our aim is not to cancel out the past, to try to forget, but to
ensure that the strength and meaning, which gave beauty to
the old pattern, is remembered and reinterpreted in the
pattern now emerging.

Colin Murray Parkes

I have always loved the following poem. I think it captures the wonder
of nature and life and gives me hope.

The Seed Shop

Here in a quiet and dusty room they lie,
Faded as crumbled stone or shifting sand,
Forlorn as ashes, shrivelled, scentless, dry
Meadows and gardens running through my hand.

In this brown husk a dale of hawthorn dreams;
A cedar in this narrow cell is thrust
That will drink deeply of a century's streams
These lilies shall make summer on my dust.

Here in this safe and simple house of death,
Sealed in their shells a million roses leap;
Here I can blow a garden with my breath,
And in my hand a forest lies asleep.

Murial Stuart

111

For Will

Thank you, my darling,
for those wonderful years,
I thought they would never end,
now I am left with just memories of you
and nursing my broken heart.

You were my soul mate,
the light of my life
my child, my priceless son,
My darling,
how could I ever imagine
your stay would not be long?

Will, please find a way to ask Jesus,
there is something I really must know,
are you happy, my darling?
please tell me that you are.
If your answer is "Yes"
and you're happy with God
Then I'll find the strength to survive.

Gill Hartley
Written for Will's 5th anniversary

Do not fear to hope....
Each time we smell the autumn's dying scent,
We know that primrose time will come again.

Samuel Taylor Coleridge

I don't know why the following poem appeals to me so much. But somehow it captures my feelings regarding the futility of all the conflict and suffering on this earth and the hope of something better to come.

Walk out of the house of time.
Walk through the paper screen of space.
Behind the party lights of stars
The fire burns without a face.

Though it is far, it is near.
It will melt your iron mind.
Much mightier than you dreamed,
But not impossible to find.

Watch your paper words in fire
How they incinerate to gold:
You are burning all your books
In the tale that can't be told.

Only then will you breathe again
In the music of the fire
And the golden dance will take you up
To the last ecstatic choir

And your wings in bliss will stretch
And the Song of Songs unfold
A symphony of blossoming
The libretto of the rose
And the cells ignite like stars
And the love like light is spread
Across the lightning circuits
Of the living and the dead

And now the walls have fallen down
And the paper's turned to dust:
The winds are free to take you,
And you must follow. You must.

Philip Wells

When it is dark enough, you can see the stars.
Ralph Waldo Emerson

Moonlight

Did you see the moon last night,
how bright it was, how clear?
strange to think
you were not born
when men first landed there.

Where were you then?

Where are you now?

Do you reside amongst the stars,
or gaze in wonder at God's face?
Or do you race as in your dream,
up alpine slopes
holding His hand and
leap like goats over mountain streams?

Whilst I am bound
by earthly cares,
I can only stop and stare
at space and wonder
where you are.

And pray one day, I'll join you there.

Gill Hartley

Candles can make us think of Christmas, we decorate our trees with electric lights now but at one time, real candles were used. Christmas can be one of the most difficult times of the year for bereaved parents to bear. So many memories of what was and can never be again. Even those parents who have surviving children will always feel sadness because of the special child who is missing. And for those of us left without children, we are so aware of the families celebrating Christmas all around us. It can be a very difficult and especially lonely time.

We will all have precious memories of the times we spent with our child or children when they were small. Christmas is, after all, a very special time for children – a magical time and as we grow older, that magic wears off. Until, that is, we have children of our own and then the excitement returns as we delight in our children's wonder at the Christmas tree, the lights and the anticipation of presents. No matter what our situation, whether we are now childless or have surviving children, the loss of a beloved child means that the celebration of Christmas can never be the same again

I will always remember carrying Will – aged eight months – into the front bedroom to watch the float carrying a waving Father Christmas, make its way along our road, with the accompanying carol singers; a procession organised by our local Round Table members, raising funds for charity. And taking Will to a local Christmas fete - a photo of him being held by the resident Father Christmas appeared in our local paper the following week. So many enchanting memories of the ensuing years – buying, wrapping and hiding the presents and Will waking, just as we used to when we were children, at the crack of dawn to open his presents.

Even before we lost Will, Christmas had lost some of its enchantment, as my niece was involved in a tragic car crash on a Christmas morning, travelling up to Lincoln to spend Christmas with her mother in law. Her husband and three-month-old baby died in the accident. But thankfully, she was young and brave enough to build a new life and is now remarried with three young children. The Christmas before Will became ill, we spent a wonderful time with my niece, nephew and their young families.

The following Christmas, everything changed. We stood by Will's bed in intensive care on Christmas Day, a day I will never forget as Will was so desperately ill. When the carol singers came round with the hospital chaplain, to sing Carols in the main ward, my mind went back to the time I stood at the window with Will as a baby, and the tears fell.

Because Will died in the middle of January, the following three Christmases were very lonely for us. It was a time of year that we came to dread. One Christmas, our fourth without Will, was different. A couple we had met from Compassionate Friends invited us to spend Christmas with them. They had also invited another mother, who would have been on her own. All of us had lost our only child. It proved to be a very special and comforting time. I know many TCF parents have found solace in sharing Christmas in this way.

We find many different ways to cope with Christmas. Those with surviving children try to have as normal a Christmas as possible, for the sake of their other children. This is difficult because whatever our circumstances, we are painfully aware that Christmas is a family time and that our family is now incomplete. Others go away, perhaps abroad, to escape the festivities. Some parents like to involve themselves in some charitable venture, such as helping serve meals to the homeless. It can be difficult for those not in our situation to understand how difficult a time this is for us, and how much support we truly need. We are painfully aware of the festivities going on around us and it can be difficult. I often feel I would like to go into hibernation over the whole period and have heard other parents say the same.

It can be so painful, seeing the shops full of Christmas goods and people in a buying frenzy. When Will was in hospital in Leicester, we were staying in a travel lodge close to the hospital. We had to go to the local shopping mall to buy some food to eat in our room, or to pick up things for Will. It was horrendous. We were surrounded by all the festive activity and it was such a contrast to the hospital environment, where so many sick people lay oblivious to all that was going on in the outside world. Having to fight our way round a crowded Tesco was the very last thing we wanted to do.

In the following poem, Eileen Whatmough captures the feeling that Christmas can never be the same again

My Christmas has been stolen,
My New Year's revelry is dust.
The tinselled trinkets
And the fairy lights
Hold no allure for me.
Watching the dancers
My leaden feet are still,
Hearing the singers
I cannot join their song.

The music stops at midnight,
The chimes, the cheers, the kisses come,
I raise my glass, I drink the toast,
But cannot share the gaiety,
Without the one I need the most.
Eileen Whatmough

We all have times we look back at with some regret and sadness. The following poem by Tony Turner captures so well the memories of the gifts

116

our children gave us, often something they had made themselves or an object that they thought was wonderful and that we would love…

A small sherry glass
I open the cupboard door,
remove a box and a glass tumbles
onto the worktop
shivers to pieces…

…and she's seven, the first
to know who Father Christmas is,
sees no reason why Mum and Dad
should have no stockings

and I'm opening mine and there
among sweets and fruit and knick-knacks
a set of sherry tumblers, a fine gold
band around each rim
scarlet huntsmen, chestnut horses,
hounds, each scene different. But how…

…from jumble sales, where value
could be had for her few pennies.
And I could have filled them all.

I'm angry now, angry with
my carelessness, I sweep up
fragments of memory,
the glass cutting me deeper
than I thought possible.

Tony Turner

Footfalls echo in the memory
Down the passage which we did not take
Towards the door we never opened

T.S. Eliot

117

I am including the following poem by Jim Denning, because it links with the frivolity of Christmas and his description of the Cherry tree seemed to link in so well with the theme of this chapter.

The Cherry Tree

(A cherry tree sometimes puts on a huge show of fruit the year before it dies, in an instinct of self-propagation. Usually we only realise this later.)

> *Where only the stump remains*
> *among the living trees*
> *we saw the cherry tree last year*
> *laden with its coming death*
> *bent beneath the heavy fruit of yesterday*
> *stuffed with sweetness*
> *its branches so curved beneath the weight*
> *the cherries of the air descended to the ground*
> *to become earth again*
> *and the white stones all around*
> *were stained with their juice.*
>
> *We saw you among us last year*
> *you who without knowing knew*
> *you would not bear again tomorrow's fruit*
> *and now we see*
> *the actions of your life are still traced out*
> *around the vanished trunk*
> *the fruit of your love*
> *remains without decay*
> *the white stones of memory*
> *come by themselves at night*
> *to shelter your dust.*
>
> **Jim Denning**

118

When we lose a beloved child, anniversaries take on a new significance. Whether it is our child's birthday, or the anniversary of the day they died, acknowledging these dates becomes profoundly important to bereaved parents. And when others do not recognise this and fail to remember, we feel hurt. I think that unless someone has experienced such a loss, they cannot understand the significance for us and the need for our child to be remembered. My mother died in 1995 and I do not feel the same need to acknowledge her birthday and the anniversary of her death, but of course I remember her especially on those days.

Will died in January 2006 and in the December of that year, Edwin and I "celebrated" our Silver wedding anniversary. We did not mark the day, it was too soon after Will and we felt unable to mark the day with anything other than sadness. The following poem was written with our anniversary in mind and Will's wonderful, silver blond hair.

Silver...

The year you died was our Silver Wedding,
but without you we could not celebrate.
Ironic you chose the name Will Silver
for your mobile and your email address.
At your funeral one of your friends told me
the girls had christened you, The Silver Fox.
We bought Silver Birch in your memory,
reflecting your lovely silver blond hair,
I bought silver white snow drops and crocus,
planted them by your stunning slate headstone
carved with silver letters bearing your name.

I will always associate silver
with you, my wonderful silver tongued son,
our love will never tarnish, it lives on...

Gill Hartley

119

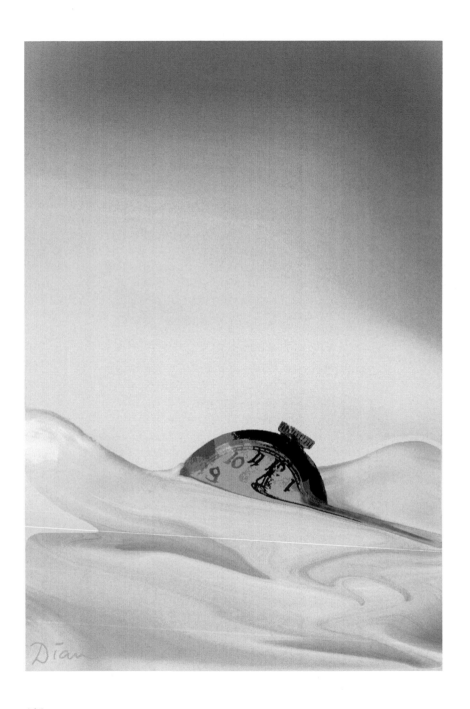

Clocks

When you get low in spirit and discouraged, remember this,
the lowest ebb is the turn of the tide.

Henry Wadsworth Longfellow

As time passes, we do change. Some of the rawness of our loss softens and although we are left with a constant sadness, we are more able to look back at the time we spent with our child and remember the good times. We are also more able to reflect on the different aspects of our grief and how it has changed us. I know I am not the person I was before Will died. I have discovered depths to my character I did not know existed, an inner strength and a deeper understanding of the needs of others. In many ways I am a nicer person. But I would forego all those changes in an instant if it meant I could have my son back. That of course can never happen and all I can do is to try to go on, to help others suffering the same kind of loss and, hopefully, make Will proud of me.

I have called this section "Clocks" because of those changes. As bereaved parents we are painfully aware of how time passes. We see friends moving on with their lives, our child's friends growing older and perhaps, depending on the age our child was, getting married and having children. Or perhaps our friends now have grandchildren and we never will.

We also get tired of being told that time heals all wounds and that, "Life goes on."

But it does go on and although time can never heal the deep wounds we bear, the pain does soften with time. Whereas in the very early days, the landscape is totally bleak, we do begin to once again see beauty around us. That said, we are hard to please. When the weather is cold and damp, I long for the warmth of Will's presence. When the weather is sunny and warm, I think he should be here to enjoy it, to sit outside a pub with his friends. I still feel the anxiety I used to feel when the forecast is for icy roads and Will had a journey to make. I then have to remind myself that particular fear is now redundant. Those feelings reflect that no matter how much time passes, we can never stop worrying about our children, whether they are still living or not. We are parents and nothing can change that.

I have always suffered from insomnia and since Will died, sleeping is even more difficult. It is hard not to think of Will lying so helpless in his hospital bed. The following poem was written many years ago, but I am including it here because I think it captures our feelings when we cannot sleep and are painfully aware that the clock ticks on, taking our beloved children further into the past...

Tick Tock

I discovered time when I was four
lying awake in my grandmother's house,
hearing the tick
and the tock
of countless clocks
some with prolonged and musical chimes,
striking not only the hour
but the half and the quarter too.
I was frightened when the clocks
struck into the night
into hours I had not known before.
For years the nightmare persisted,
hopelessly running to catch my mother,
forever aware of the slow ticking clock,
as she walked down a parallel street.

I would anger my father in later years:
creeping downstairs to stop the hall clock,
stilling the pendulum so it could not strike
and tick-tock insomnia into the night.

Gill Hartley

Time is

Too Slow for those who Wait,
Too Swift for those who Fear,
Too Long for those who Grieve,
Too Short for those who Rejoice;
But for those who Love,
Time is Not.

Henry Van Dyke

In this section, I have endeavoured to bring together a collection of prose and poetry which captures some of those thoughts and feelings as we look back and long for all we have lost.

> *"They are not long, the weeping and the laughter,*
> *Love and desire and hate:*
> *I think they have no portion in us after*
> *We pass the gate.*
> *They are not long, the days of wine and roses:*
> *Out of a misty dream*
> *Our path emerges for awhile, then closes*
> *Within a dream."*
>
> **Ernest Dowson**

In the very early days of our loss, we feel guilty if we catch ourselves laughing or smiling at something. I think humour is invaluable and can help us hold on during those desperate days. When my mother died, one of the nurses from the "stay at home" hospice caring for her said that anyone going into their office would be shocked at the laughter. I replied that I wouldn't because in a profession like theirs, when you are faced with constant sadness, humour is a vital safety valve.

And so it is with us. I often thank God for giving us humour, something we, as bereaved parents, are much in need of. Not long after Will died, totally alone one day and in need of some love and understanding, I was pleased to receive a phone call from a friend offering me some figs from the tree in her garden and asking if I would like to walk round to her house to collect them. When I arrived, she met me at the door, thrust a bowl of very ripe figs into my hands and said she could not stop to talk because, (a) she hadn't had lunch yet, and (b) she had a friend from church coming to talk with her about pastoral care. As I walked away, I could almost see Will grinning wryly at me - the irony of the situation would not have escaped his attention.

"If I didn't laugh, I'd cry," my mother used to say this to describe something so ironic that you had a choice; you laughed or you cried. Will had a wonderful sense of humour, very dry and observant. At first meeting, people may have thought him to be a serious young man, but once they got to know him, they looked for the twinkle in his eyes and wanted to share whatever it was he had found amusing.

A sorrow's crown of sorrow is remembering happier times.
Alfred Lord Tennyson

Even when Will was in hospital, there were times when we laughed with him and his sense of humour was there, despite his suffering. I remember on one occasion Will got the giggles when one of the doctors was describing the huge steins the waitress carried – one in each hand – at the beer festival in Germany. Our osteopath, who over the years had become a good friend, came to visit Will. He and Will had always got on very well and could always make one another laugh. Will was very ill when Gareth came, although we did not know it at the time it was only a few days before he died.

When Will saw Gareth, he asked for his writing pad to be held for him and wrote the words, "Don't make me laugh". Gareth was putting a cold cloth on Will's forehead to help reduce his temperature. Suddenly Will put his hand up, took the cloth of his head and wrung the excess water out onto the floor. The poor nurse was so alarmed when she heard the sound of the water! It made us all smile, even at a time like that.

Mister God, this is Anna, is a very moving book about a remarkable child called Anna. In her short life Anna had a huge impact on the lives of everyone who met her, not least because of her unshakeable faith in God and her closeness to Him. We cannot but smile at her wonderful way with words.

When I shall die,
I shall do it myself.
Nobody shall do it for me.
When I am ready,
I shall say,
"Fin, stand me up",
and I shall look
and laugh merry.
If I fall down,
I shall be dead.
From "Mr God, this is Anna"

They say such nice things about people at their funerals that it makes me sad that I'm going to miss mine by just a few days.
Garrison Keillor

124

A friend from TCF, whose only son died in an accident, made us smile when she told us how she had stayed with a friend and they had gone shopping together. One of the shops they visited was a shoe shop and she had tried on a pair but did not buy them. When she got into her car to drive home, she saw a pair of shoes in the car that did not match each other. She realised then that she had worn an odd pair of shoes the entire day and wondered what the assistant in the shoe shop must have thought!

Despite finding we can smile without experiencing the guilt we experience in the early days of our loss, we still feel deep and enduring sadness when we think back to what was and we long for everything to be restored.

I love the following poem by Diane Shepherd. It captures so well the emotion we experience when we realise just how the years have passed and our longing for what used to be can be as intense as ever it was.

Three Visits

Visit 1   *Long sad years*
since you died.
So many tears
since you died.
Every day tinged with pain.
Life's gone on
sunshine, rain.
Living, loving, laughing -
keeping emotion inside.
But oh! My dear one
how I've cried
and it's the day before, the day before
you died.

Visit 2   *I've come to know this place so well*
since you died.
My place for contemplation
since you died.
I mean to join you –
who can tell?

I carry on, the best I can –
adrift, adrift with no real plan.
But oh! My dear one
how I've cried.
And it's the day before
you died.

Visit 3   *Long sad years*
since you died.
So many tears
since you died.
Today just empty
tears safely contained,
So little of you remained –
after you left us and went.
Emotion, mine, spent.
But oh! My dear one
how I've cried.
And it's the day,
today is the day –
You died ...

                                    Diane Shepherd

Presentiment
August is baleful,
full of thunder and omens
breathing on my skin.

Wrapped in newsprint
I nurse the cold in my head.
Only the sound of the rain
seeps through.

Lulled by library books
ad linctus, I wait,

remembering past summers,
their small bereavements,
smells of burning,
London street hot
and empty as these fields.

Then the shadows fall
as the month turns,
as the page turns
to the dark calendar
hooked in my heart.

Pat Sentinella

My thoughts are chalices of sand;
Your memory floods them and I weep.
Ethel M. Hewitt *from Heart's Tide*

Will and I always enjoyed feeding and observing the birds in our garden. Shortly before Will became ill, we had gone up to Norfolk together for week. Whilst there, we visited some of the RSPB reserves and bought new feeders for our garden. Since Will died, I have found some comfort in continuing to feed the birds but, to my dismay, we are plagued by two neighbouring cats, both of whom are excellent hunters. The following poem reflects my anger and sadness.

Obsession

I bankrupt myself feeding birds,
buying birdseed, mealworms and feeders,
furnish the garden with shrubs
create a wildlife reserve.
I watch from the window entranced
at the spectacle of spring,
the garden is full of burgeoning life,
baby birds on the wing.
There should be pleasure in this,
bringing comfort to a wounded heart,
the knowledge that life does go on
and I can play my small part.
But, as before, I am cheated by death,
that stalks unbidden, unseen:
creeping cats in the undergrowth,
or cruelly launched from the sky.
Like cats, the sparrow hawk cannot lose,

takes innocence by surprise.
Distressed by the grief of the parent birds
and my failure to protect or forestall,
I am left angry, bereft and grieving,
for death makes fools of us all.

Gill Hartley

This poem makes me think of how closely our lives can be entwined with animals. Many of us have a dog or a cat that may have been our child's pet. When the time comes when we have to part with that pet, maybe through old age or illness, it can be a very painful experience.

When we found our beautiful border collie, Luke, had inoperable cancer, we had to make the hard decision to have him put to sleep. I had dreaded something happening to Luke as he was such a strong link to Will. For some months following Will's death I was unable to walk with Luke on my own. I had an irrational fear that something might happen to him, he might get into a fight and be hurt or he might get lost. After a while, these fears abated and walking with him was one of my lifelines. Walking through the woods with Luke came to provide me with much solace and at such times I felt very close to Will.

I wrote the following article for the Compassionate Friends journal, shortly after dear Luke was put to sleep, in the hope that other parents who had to make the decision to part with their dead child's pet, would identify with what I had written.

A hard decision

I scrunch my fingers into the soft warm fur around Luke's neck, stroke and kiss his head. I whisper to him what a wonderful friend. I tell him he will see Will. There is a momentary arch of his body, very slight, almost imperceptible. He is so relaxed, so comfortable. I turn to look at Mark, who is kneeling beside me, the syringe in his hand. "Is that it?" I say but I already know that it is. Luke is lying, his head still against the arm of the couch, his eyes still half closed. He looks so peaceful. I want to wake him up, say "Come on Luke, let's go for a walk".

He had his last walk this afternoon, an hour or so before Mark arrived. It was almost like old times. We took him across the cricket ground and into the field beyond. Luke scampered about, sniffing, enjoying himself, a happy, healthy dog, out for a walk with his owners. No one observing him could ever have suspected there was anything wrong, there was nothing in his behaviour to indicate, as we had discovered the previous day, that Luke was a very sick dog, riddled with a deadly cancer.

With Luke's death, the utter finality of all that we have lost, has hit me with unexpected force. I had always anticipated that losing Luke would be difficult. In many ways he was the last living link with our son, Will, and with Luke's death a whole chapter of our lives has closed forever. We are aware now, more than ever before, of the finality of Will's death.

I already owned a border collie when I met Edwin and throughout Will's lifetime we always had a dog. Now the house seems so empty and the silence haunts me. The door bell rings and there is no Luke barking madly – I often opened the door before callers had time to ring the doorbell, joking that we did not need a doorbell when we had Luke. If a package were being delivered, Luke would bark excitedly outside my son's room. He knew I would shut him in there whilst opening the door. He alerted me to the phone ringing too – useful if I was out in the garden or somewhere out of earshot.

I often wonder just how much Luke understood about Will. We are only just beginning to realise just how intelligent and aware our canine friends are and medical researchers are learning how dogs can be used to detect certain illnesses in humans. I wonder too whether witnessing our grief for Will and his own grief for him triggered Luke's cancer. So often, especially in the early days, he would go up to young men when we were out walking – I often thought he was looking for Will. And it was to Will's room that Luke would retreat when he was frightened by fireworks or during a thunderstorm and he continued to do this right up to the time of his own death.

Since Will died, Luke has been my reason to get up in the morning. I am not a creature of habit but walking Luke around the same time every morning seemed vital to me. I found walking *with him very therapeutic. He got me out in all weathers and we enjoyed long walks together, to a nearby country park, local woodlands or walks by the river. Since Luke's death, I have lingered in bed every morning, reluctant to start the day, reluctant to go downstairs and not have Luke to greet me. It is as if my grief for Will has intensified with the loss of Luke. So many memories; all those walks with the two of them, holidays, Will playing with Luke, Will snuggling up with Luke, Luke jumping up on Will's bed. So many memories, such precious times. The tears keep falling and I cannot make them stop. How much more will be taken from me? How much more can I survive? I want the world to stop. Now.*

Sometime, in the not too distant future, we will adopt another rescue border collie, maybe, in time, two of them. But it is an odd thought that the new dog will never be a part of Will's life or visa versa. And with this thought comes the knowledge that we are taking yet another step into a future we never envisaged – a future without our son.

Six months later we did adopt another rescued Border Collie. And it did feel strange to know he would never know Will. But he has brought his own character with him and although it took me a while to adjust to him, he now has a place in our home and our hearts.

Yesterday, Today and Tomorrow

There are two days in every week about which we should not worry -

Two days which can be kept free from fear and apprehension.

One of these days is Yesterday with its mistakes and cares, its ashes and pains, its faults and blunders. Yesterday has passed forever beyond our control. All the money in the world cannot bring it back. We cannot undo a single act we performed; we cannot erase a single word we said. Yesterday is gone.

The other day we would do well not to worry about is Tomorrow – with its adversities, its burdens, its large promise and poor performance. Tomorrow is also beyond our immediate control. Tomorrow's sun will rise either in splendour or behind a mask of

130

clouds – but it will rise. Until it does, we have no stake in Tomorrow, for it is yet unborn.

That leaves only one day – Today. Any person can fight the battles of just one day. It is only when you and I add the burdens of these two awful eternities – Yesterday and Tomorrow – that we break down.

It is not the experience of Today, which drives people mad – it is remorse or bitterness for something that happened Yesterday and the dread of what Tomorrow may bring.

Let us, therefore, journey but one day at a time...

Author unknown

When we first lost Will I hoped that when we met with other bereaved parents we would derive assurance from them that after the first dreadful year, we would begin to feel a bit "better". I am thankful to the other parents we met, some several years "ahead" of us, who warned us that the second year would be worse and the following one, worse still. I can remember thinking that was impossible; I could not feel any worse than I did at that time. Now I understand. We are in shock for much longer than we realise, in fact we can remain in a state of relative numbness for some years. In Barbara Rosof's excellent book, The Worst Loss, she writes,

"Many parents, during the second or third year, felt a shift in their awareness. They felt, to a degree that they had not experienced before, the utter finality of their loss. Nothing could ever be done to undo the death of their child and to fill the empty space it had left in their lives. It would be with them forever."

She goes on to say that this shift in understanding, or the deepening of it, reflects the magnitude of their loss; that all that a parent loses when their child dies is too much to take in at one time. One parent she talks of describes it as being like falling down a very long flight of stairs. He says, *"You fall a few steps and you land sprawled on your face on the landing. You rest there awhile and then, never when you're ready, you start falling again. This time you fall farther. You know more what you have lost".*

Time Does Not Bring Relief

Time does not bring relief; you all have lied
Who told me time would ease me of my pain!
I miss him in the weeping of the rain;
I want him at the shrinking of the tide;
The old snows melt from every mountain-side,
And last year's leaves are smoke in every lane;
But last year's bitter loving must remain
Heaped on my heart, and my old thoughts abide.
There are a hundred places where I fear
To go,—so with his memory they brim.
And entering with relief some quiet place
Where never fell his foot or shone his face
I say, "There is no memory of him here!"
And so stand stricken, so remembering him.

Edna St. Vincent Millay

I sometimes hold it half a sin
   To put into the words I feel;
   For words, like nature, half reveal
And half conceal the soul within.

But for the unquiet heart and brain,
   A use in measured language lies;
   The sad mechanic exercise,
Like dull narcotics, numbing pain.

In word, like weeds, I'll wrap me o'er
   Like coarsest clothes against the cold:
   But that large grief which these enfold
Is given in outline and no more.

Alfred, Lord Tennyson
From In Memoriam, A.H.

132

I measure every grief I meet
With narrow, probing, eyes,
I wonder if it weighs like mine
Or has an easier size.

I wonder if they bore it long
Or did it just begin,
I could not tell the date of mine
It feels so old a pain.

I wonder if it hurts to live
And if they have to try
And whether – could they choose between -
It would not be to die.

I note that some, gone patient long,
At length, renew their smile,
An imitation of a light
That has so little oil –

I wonder if when years have piled –
Some thousands on the harm
That hurt them early, such a lapse
Could give them any balm.

Or would they go on aching still
Through centuries of nerve
Enlightened to a larger pain
In contrast with the love.

The grieved are many I am told
There is the various cause
Death is but one and comes but once
And only nails the eyes.

There's grief of want and grief of cold,
A sort they call "despair"
There's banishment from native eyes
In sight of native air.

And though I may not guess the kind
Correctly, yet to me
A piercing comfort it affords
In passing Calvary.

To note the fashions of the Cross
And how they're mostly worn
Still fascinated to presume
That some are like my own

Emily Dickenson

Losing Will was the single most traumatic event in my life and I will miss him every second of every day. I don't know if my poems have changed, maybe they are more reflective now.

My grief for Will has not lessened. What has happened is that I am learning to live with the pain, it is part of me. The following poem reflects feelings just as strong and powerful as when Will first died.

Pain

I hoped the pain would ease with time,
and I would, as many people said,
"Move on"
"Feel better"
"Get over" you.

Now I know these clichés are false
and all too glibly are expressed
by those who cannot possibly know
time will not heal a wound like this.
There is no remedy on earth
to heal a broken heart and soul.

For when you died and left for Heaven,
my soul was wrenched from me
and it will never find its home
until my body dies and sets it free
to find its place in Heaven with you
and we become the soul-mates we used to be.

Gill Hartley

Sue White's eighteen-year old son, Paul, died in a car accident. Sue describes her feelings as she reflects on the twelve years since Paul died.

I am now facing twelve years without Paul and I do not know how I have got here. On the day Paul died, did I close my eyes in pain and fear and it has taken me all this time to open them again and see the world as it is now. Or did I blink as I was told Paul had died and all those years vanished in a haze of despair and confusion. If my mind had taken the full impact of Paul's loss in those first moments, would I be here at all?

It is strange that sometimes it feels as though it was just yesterday that Paul died. My pain is unbearable and I can feel him as he kissed me goodbye that morning and turned at the gate and bequeathed me a beautiful smile. At other times it can seem like forever, or that he never really existed and I conjured up this beautiful boy and all he became.

Reality is that Paul did exist but that he is with me in a very different way now. Sometimes, that is enough and the warmth of his love will spread throughout my veins and we are closer than we could ever have been. It is as though I have managed to take him back inside me as he once was before he was born and we are one.

Then there are times when living without him is unbearable, the pain as raw as those early moments, only worse somehow because the years have blunted and softened the edges and I have forgotten how I can be brought to my knees with the agony of losing him.

My memories are there, but hidden beneath the debris of his loss and often need to be provoked by a photograph. For years I had no memories. The shock of his loss hid everything that existed before that day and no matter how I tried I could not salvage any moment at all between my birth and Paul's death. I learned to live for each moment as there seemed to be no past to hold onto and a future I could not bear to face.

The years have passed in a blur of pain and despair. Every moment on the early path of grief was fought against with a fear of forgetting Paul, of losing him from my mind as well as the physical loss I was enduring. It is only time that has taught me that the pain must be worked through, that each time I thought I was losing a little more of Paul he was taking his place inside me.

I think I am now as content as I can be without Paul. I no longer expect to change very much how I feel about Paul's death and being without him has become something I must live with all my life. I miss the physical Paul all the time but he is so much a part of me now that there feels no separation in my mind.

I live with a constant sadness which sits alongside the joys that life still brings. The legacy Paul left me is seeing the world through new eyes – the healing power of nature; understanding that love is everything and a release from the shallow worries that are no longer important enough to feature in my life.

A coat for all seasons

My coat is not in fashion
It has no colour and no shape
It is heavy on my body
No season can escape

It covers me when bulbs
Force the earth to breathe spring air
It hangs a listless burden
When the summer sun is here

In autumn when the leaves fall
Or when winter's earth is still
It clings in bulky layers
Giving out no heat at all

It doesn't take up any space
Needs no cleaning and no care
You may not see me wearing it
That doesn't mean it isn't there

I have had my coat for many years
I have settled in its folds
Fashions come and fashions go
But I'll wear it 'til I'm old

I cannot say I love my coat
But without it you would see
Just what the pain of losing Paul
Has really done to me

© Sue White

Diane Shepherd's younger son, Dan, died in a car accident in 1998 at the age of twenty-seven. Several of Diane's thoughtful poems appear in this book.

Gone too soon

I know you can never come back again –
How clearly my eyes now see.
Whatever the season, sunshine or rain
Thoughts of you always return to me.

The kindness of your eyes,
The touch of your hand,
Those elements of surprise,
The way you would stand.

So many thoughts of you I have each day
How straight you were, how tall, how strong.
No one can reach me in just your way,
Every day of my life –
Your absence ...so wrong...

Diane Shepherd

Will used to tease me and call me a "silver surfer" when it came to using the Internet to buy anything. I wish he could see me now. I now buy most of my clothes and Edwin's via the Internet as I still find shopping stressful.

I also find I still avoid some of the places I strongly associate with Will. This is hard for others to understand and people often say that they "think I should". I wish it were that simple. I am still trying to cope with the reality of Will's death and to go to some of those places I know would cause me too much pain. There is a cottage garden nursery in the Cotswolds that Will and I used to visit together. The last time we went there was on my birthday – the last birthday Will and I were to spend together. It was a very special day.

I will never forget our beautiful border collie, Luke, sitting in the back of the car surrounded by the plants that Will had so carefully tucked into every available space. We had lunch in a lovely old pub, sitting in the shade with Luke. It was a wonderful day. I could never have imagined it would never happen again...

End of Summer

Leaves falling –
Autumn approaches.
Spirits lifted when summer warmth was here.
And now?
Strength to find for myself
Strength to find for others,
And nothing left for you.
Just love...
Just longing...

Diane Shepherd

Dried grass in winter

Here are the husks,
ghosts of summer.

A haunting of hare's tail,
sweet vernal,

yellow oat, meadow soft,
wall barley.

Slender stalks snapped from the root.
Dry statements

wild and sad
with their weight of grief.

These the straws
that will break her.

Pat Sentinella

in the end
you still
live
in me
like clouds
in a vernal pond
whose sky
has vanished

Chris Agee

Clowns

Oh, would that man had not invented time
It cannot take our deepest pain away
We are all clowns and life's a pantomime.

Time's just a word and it's a paradigm
Of man's desire to keep the truth at bay
Oh, would that man had not invented time.

If you believe that life's all summertime
And all we have to do is laugh and play
We are all clowns and life's a pantomime.

We listen to the clock's relentless chime
And hope the hurt will ease with each new day
Oh, would that man had not invented time.

We so want to believe our lives will rhyme
With happiness and life will not decay
We are all clowns and life's a pantomime

If mountains were not there for us to climb
We'd play it safe and watch the matinee
Oh, would that man had not invented time
We are all clowns and life's a pantomime.

Gill Hartley

Through a glass darkly

For now we see through a glass, darkly; but then face to face: now I
know in part; but then shall I know even as also I am known.
I Corinthians 13 v 12

Although I have struggled with my faith since Will died, I still hold onto my Christian beliefs. Will's faith was very strong and his uncompromising faith helps me to go on living without him.

I often recall a conversation Will and I had one evening, some time ago, when he said, "If anything ever happened to me, Mum, you shouldn't worry because you'd know where I'd be." Then he added, "And I'd know where you'd be too, if anything happened to you." I can remember my reply, "Well, I know where you'd be Will, but I'm not so sure about me." Will said, "You just don't get it Mum, do you?" Maybe I didn't then but I know what he meant. It is a matter of trust and choice. I hold on to that memory and other experiences both Will and I had since becoming Christians and it does give me the strength to go on.

Edwin, who now would his describe his faith as "dormant" when Will became ill, found his faith during those traumatic days. One evening in our small Travelodge room, just after I had been praying with him for Will, Edwin came and knelt beside the bed and wept. He said he felt it was all his fault (it wasn't of course but one of the horrible feelings that assail us when we feel so utterly helpless as parents) and that he could not find the words to pray. I said to him that it didn't matter, because at such times, St Paul writes that the Holy Spirit intercedes on our behalf with groans and sighs to God. Reaching for my Bible to read the relevant passage, we were both shaken when the book opened at the very page I was about to look for. I read the passage to Edwin and then tentatively suggested he pray the prayer of submission to Jesus, inviting Him into his life. And so Will's dearest wish for his father came true. There, kneeling by my bed, Edwin repeated the words after me and gave his life to Jesus. Recalling this moment brings tears to my eyes, especially when we told Will the next day what had happened. He looked at Edwin and smiled, then put his hand to his chest and mouthed the words, "Because of me?" "Yes", we said, "Because of you."

Although, as I said in the opening paragraph, I have struggled with my faith since Will died, Edwin doesn't and his strong belief has helped to keep me going without our precious son.

I can well understand why many bereaved parents turn away from God in their grief and anger. When a bereaved mother says to me that she does not believe in God, I often reply, "But what else do we have?" The alternative is too awful to contemplate. I don't think I would cope being here without Will if I did not have the hope and belief that I will be with him again one day.

> *I stand one side of the bridge that divides -*
> *the water is deep and filled with despair,*
> *there's no way to cross over to your side,*
> *the bridge is too fragile and beyond repair,*
> *it will not survive the weight of my pain -*
> *I have no choice but to live without you;*
> *the long lonely years alone I'll remain.*
> *My darling, there is nothing else I can do,*
> *but pray to God and ask Him to lead me*
> *through this dark valley of sadness and fear,*
> *to where He abides and where you will be -*
> *where God sets us free and dries all our tears.*
> *There we will dwell in the light of His grace,*
> *then at last, at last, we will see His face...*
>
> **Gill Hartley**

The times when I struggle with my faith, my anger at God at the seeming unfairness of it all overwhelms me. A Christian leader talks of what he calls "The betrayal barrier" and how often committed Christians, when faced with such devastating and unfathomable circumstances, feel abandoned by God. The following words, taken from a longer poem, connected with my grief and anger and it was a poem I read over and over again.

> *Yes, faith is a goodly anchor;*
> *When skies are as sweet as a psalm,*
> *At the bows it lolls so stalwart,*
> *In its bluff, broad shouldered calm....*

But after the shipwreck, tell me
What help in its iron thews,
Still true to the broken hawser'
Deep down among seaweed and ooze?

In the breaking gulfs of sorrow,
When the helpless feet stretch out
And find in the deeps of darkness
No footing as solid as doubt.

Then better one spar of Memory
One broken plank of the Past,
That our human heart may cling to,
Though hopeless of shore at last!

Immortal? I feel it and know it,
Who doubts it of such as she?
But that is the pang's very secret -
Immortal away from me.

There's a narrow ridge in the graveyard
Would scarce stay a child in its race,
But to me and my thought it is wider
Than the star-sown vague of Space.

Your logic, my friend, is perfect,
Your moral most drearily true;
But, since the earth clashed on her coffin,
I keep hearing that and not you.

Console if you will, I can bear it;
'Tis a well meant alms of breath;
But not all the teaching since Adam
Has made Death other than Death.

It is pagan, but wait till you feel it,-
That jar of our earth, that dull shock
When the ploughshare of deeper passion
Tears down to our primitive rock.

Communion in spirit! Forgive me,
But I, who am earthly and weak,
Would give all my incomes from dreamland
For a touch of her hand on my cheek.
                                    James Russell Lowell

Will was my soul mate; we were unusually close and only had to look at one another to know what the other one was thinking. I could not envisage a future without him and still cannot believe this has happened. A friend kindly gave me a beautiful book of prose and poetry for Will's first anniversary and one night I read a line from the book to my husband: "We do not understand the meaning of the word final until final is final." My husband said the following night that the words kept coming back to him. It is the finality that is so hard to accept. Although I try to hold on to the belief I will see Will again one day, it does not take away the pain of having to live the rest of my life here without him. When Will was first in hospital and we were aware of how serious his condition was, I remember hurling my Bible at the rubbish bin, saying that I could not live without Will and did not even want to try. I felt completely isolated and abandoned by God and in one sense I still do. I have been surprised at how angry I can feel; anger at God; anger with people who do not understand, anger with myself. At times I fear I am losing my faith. But deep down, I know it is still there – in fact one of the factors that have prevented me from taking my own life, is that I can imagine Will saying, "What are you doing here, Mum?" That, and knowing I must stay for my husband and the dog, (although my husband always says it's the other way round!)

This beautiful hymn never fails to make me cry. Both Will and I loved it and a stunning version of it was played at Will's funeral service. Will always loved the thought he was one of God's sons and we chose words from this hymn to be carved around the rim of the simple slate headstone we commissioned for Will's grave. I also called my first book, My True Son, because of this hymn.

Be Thou my Vision, O Lord of my heart;
Naught be all else to me, save that Thou art.
Thou my best Thought, by day or by night,
Waking or sleeping, Thy presence my light.

Be Thou my Wisdom, and Thou my true Word;
I ever with Thee and Thou with me, Lord;
Thou my great Father, I Thy true son;
Thou in me dwelling, and I with Thee one.

Be Thou my battle Shield, Sword for the fight;
Be Thou my Dignity, Thou my Delight;
Thou my soul's Shelter, Thou my high Tower:
Raise Thou me heavenward, O Power of my power.

Riches I heed not, nor man's empty praise,
Thou mine Inheritance, now and always:
Thou and Thou only, first in my heart,
High King of Heaven, my Treasure Thou art.

High King of Heaven, my victory won,
May I reach Heaven's joys, O bright Heaven's Sun!
Heart of my own heart, whatever befall,
Still be my Vision, O Ruler of All.

Lord be My Vision, Book of the Gael

When I went to the Anglican convent to seek some comfort, shortly after Will died, the lovely nun whom I talked with told me that she had always had three major fears in her life, one was a fear of dying because she believed she was "not good enough" for God, the second was a fear of the dentist and the third a fear of cancer. As it turned out, she told me, she had to face all of her fears at once when she was diagnosed with cancer of the tongue. During surgery she had a near death experience, which had changed her perception of death and resolved her fears. Although she could not remember the details of what she had seen, her enduring memory was the realisation that all the unanswered questions suddenly made sense and she could remember thinking, "Ah, now I see..." I don't think she was meant to remember what the unanswered questions were but what was clear was her deep assurance that, one day, everything would make sense and we would understand why.

Our God of Hope

There is a God whose light shines in every darkness
There is a God who hears every lament
There is a God who transforms even the deepest grief
Therefore you have hope:
You shall sing again, but with a different tune
You shall dance again, but with a different step
You shall laugh again, but with a different breath
Not yet, but one day,
For there is a God who heals your wound
with the gentlest hand.

Michael Mitton

The Weaver was read at a special service in our church the Sunday following Will's death. Edwin and I were still in Nottingham with my cousin. It was only when we returned home that we learned that our vicar and our curate had completely reorganised the Sunday service to comfort a stunned congregation who had for the last six weeks been praying for Will's healing. Opinions vary as to who wrote the poem. Some find the words comforting, others don't and disagree with the sentiments expressed. I find that it helps to lock into my belief that there is a purpose to all the suffering and I hope and trust that one day it will all make sense.

The Weaver

My life is just a weaving
Between my Lord and me.
I cannot choose the colours
He weaves so skillfully.

Sometimes He weaveth sorrow
And I in foolish pride

Forget He sees the upper
And I the underside.

Not 'til the loom is silent
And the shuttles cease to fly
Will God unroll the canvas
And explain the reasons why -

The dark threads are as needful,
In The Weaver's skilful hands
As the threads of gold and silver
In the pattern He has planned.
Benjamin Malachi Franklin

The following article was written by Ian Campbell and appeared in the Summer 2009 edition of The Compassionate Friends' journal, Compassion. It is reprinted below with Ian's kind permission.

Blind Faith

Not long ago I got into a conversation about religion in a pub. A friend remarked that he really admired people like me with blind faith. I stopped him and said I objected to 'blind' always being put in front of faith, presumably to contrast it with the clear-eyed reason of agnosticism or atheism. I pointed out that I had not always been a practising Christian and had become one only at the age of 25 after years of reasoning and reflection. I came to believe that the Resurrection was the most reasonable explanation to account for what happened after the death of Jesus, and that the logical consequence of this belief was to join a church.

However, since that conversation, I have been thinking and realise that there is a large element of blindness in my faith or trust in God but that has not always been the case. Jesus tells us in the Gospels that every hair on our heads has been counted by God and that not even a single sparrow falls to the ground without God knowing about it. I believe I have to try to trust that everything that happens to me is according to God's will but I have never been very good at doing so. The hardest test was when my nine-year old son, Hugh, died in November 2000, after falling off his bike for no apparent reason.

147

One famous prayer that I discovered after I became a Catholic has always stuck in my throat. It was written by St Ignatius Loyola, founder of the Jesuits:

Take, Lord, and receive all my liberty, my memory, my understanding, and my entire will – all that I have and call my own. You have given it all to me. To you, Lord, I return it. Everything is yours; do with it what you will. Give me only your love and your grace. That is enough for me.

I could imagine, or at least hope, that I would be prepared to give up my own life if God demanded it but I could not include my two sons in 'all that I have and call my own'. That was asking too much.

A few weeks after Hugh's death, two things happened on the same day. The first, in the morning, was that we received a message of condolence, written on the back of a postcard showing a detail of beautiful contemporary stained glass window from the monastery of Taizé in Burgundy. It showed a young boy, whom I first thought was an angel, but then I noticed that what I had taken for wings were actually hands resting on the boy's shoulders. I turned the card over to find out the subject. It was Isaac, which meant that the hands must be those of his father, Abraham. In one of the most horrifying stories in the Bible God tests Abraham's faith to the limits by telling him to take his young son to a distant mountain and there to sacrifice him. Abraham does all that God commanded and gets as far as raising the knife to kill Isaac when an angel intervenes. I could never identify with Abraham's unquestioning submission to the will of God, but that afternoon, I was listening to Choral Evensong on Radio 3, and the first reading was that very same story. It then struck me that something not dissimilar had happened to me: God had taken away my son and left me my faith. It gave me no comfort. I often feel that it would be easier not to have to believe in an all-loving, all-powerful and all-knowing God, who let my son die. Yet, the fact of Hugh's death and my belief in the Resurrection are two separate things. His death is no different in essence from those of countless other innocent people, who died in accidents or natural catastrophes, 'Acts of God'. If their deaths do not shake the core of my faith, why should Hugh's? Whatever my feelings of anger and desolation, to go on doggedly trusting in God is an act of will, which I can choose to exercise even when blinded by grief.

Reason can only take me so far along the road. There are areas of darkness where its light cannot penetrate and then I have to rely on faith. But faith does not mean not having doubts. Just as the absence of fear is not courage but recklessness, so the absence of doubt is not faith but credulity. We are only brave when we feel frightened but do not let the fear overwhelm us. Likewise, I am faithful if I do not let the siren voices of doubt erode my trust.

In the weeks after Hugh died, I scoured the Bible to try to make sense of his death and to sustain my faith. Among the countless reiterations of 'Do not be afraid' (the commonest phrase in the Bible) and reassurances that God loves us and wants good things for us, I kept coming back to Isaiah ch. 55 vv. 8-9:

For my thoughts are not your thoughts, neither are your ways my ways, says the Lord. For as the heavens are higher than the earth, so are my ways higher than your ways and my thoughts than your thoughts.

These words are not at first hearing consoling. They may even sound crushing, dismissing our futile attempts to understand 'Acts of God'. But, the bottom line is that we must take God's promises on trust, even if they appear utterly incomprehensible from our human perspective.

And, nine years on, looking back I can see that my faith has given me consolation, and even quiet underlying joy that I don't think I was so aware of before Hugh's death. I have to accept that, however much I believe my faith in God is reasonable; I will never make sense of his death this side of the grave, or much else that happens in the world. I accept also that it may turn out when I die that I am wrong and there is nothing. But until then all I can do is hold on to faith, which I am now prepared to acknowledge is, ultimately, blind.

Ian Campbell

At the funeral service of a young friend who had died suddenly leaving four young children, the author, Pete Greig, watched one of the young daughters staring at her father's coffin, whilst the rest of the congregation sang and celebrated his friend's life. Pete reflected, *"how fragile our faith must be if we can't remain sad, scared, confused and doubting for a while."*

C S Lewis's much loved books for children, The Chronicles of Narnia, carry a strong message of Christian hope. The following extract I have included because when Digory pleads with Aslan, he realises when he sees the tears in Aslan's eyes, that the great lion shared his pain. We have to believe that God does share our pain and, as he promised, one day He will wipe away all our tears.

"But please, please – won't you – can't you give me something that will cure mother?" Up till then he had been looking at the Lion's great feet and the huge claws on them; now, in his despair, he looked up at its face. What he saw surprised him as much as anything else in his whole life. For the tawny face was bent down near his own and (wonder of wonders) great shining tears stood in the Lion's eyes. They were such big, bright tears compared with Digory's own that for a moment he felt as if the Lion must really be sorrier about his mother than he was himself.

C S Lewis: *The Magician's Nephew*

Most of us hold on to the hope that one day we will be reunited with our beloved child or children. As a Christian I believe that Will is safe and happy where he is now. The following poems reflect something of that hope.

Deluge
I'm wedged on a ledge beneath a waterfall.
The ledge is narrow, and if I edge forward,
I will be certain to fall.
Although drawn to death, I am distracted
by joyous sights in the tumbling stream,
the mist from which forms sequins of water,
that dance in the spangled shafts of light.

Voices as soft as sunlight echo from the cliff,
singing songs of pure delight.
I fear they will drown in the deluge of water
but don't souls live on and never die?

Gill Hartley

Good is that darkening of our lives,
Which only God can brighten;
But better still that hopeless load,
Which none but God can lighten.

Rev. Frederick William Fabe

We are born for a higher destiny that that of earth.
There is a realm where the rainbow never fades,
Where the stars will be spread out before us like the islands
That slumber on the ocean and where the beautiful beings that
Have passed before us like visions will stay in our presence forever.

Author unknown

Though nothing can bring back the hour
Of splendour in the grass, of glory in the flower;
We will grieve not, rather find
Strength in what remains behind.

William Wordsworth

Some years ago, Will and I travelled to Zakepone in Poland. Realising that we were not far from the infamous Auschwitz and learning that there was a coach trip visiting the camp the following day, we felt compelled to go. It was an experience neither of us could forget but one which we did not regret making. I wrote the following poems after our visit and somehow they seem to fit into the theme of this book. So many unanswered questions...

Amber

In Krakow we bought amber,
combed the honey-laden shops,
fingering necklaces, brooches,
rings, the amber warm,
almost soft, to our touch.
Jewellery made
from a harvest of tears.

My purchase was costly
although the amber was cheap
cheap, unless set in gold.
My sleeve was caught
as I left the shop, by a gypsy
with a child in her arms.

She waited as I fumbled for a coin,
the necklace in my handbag,
now cold, like a stone.
When she smiled her thanks at me
I caught a glimpse of gold.

In my room that evening,
I thought of a place we had seen
and of jewellery made
out of mortuary gold,
and like amber,
from a harvest of tears.

Gill Hartley

Peter

We could have been almost anywhere,
at any museum in the world.
Part of a group, with a guide
whose faultless patter lulled us
from one display to the next.
And as always, on such occasions,
I felt the weight of fatigue.

Appalled, I moved away from the group
and perhaps to provoke some sense of reality,
I sought out singular things.
Like a still blonde plait, amid the awful hoard
of greyed, decaying hair.
And the small brown case that was Peter's.
So similar to the countless others,
each daubed with a name and date of birth.
"Peter Heulch. 23 11 42."
One of our party said,
she'd visited all of the camps.
She said no birds fly at Belsen.
There were birds at Auschwitz, I know
because I looked for them.
But at Auschwitz - Birkenau,
no birds sang at all.
Wild flowers failed to soften
the monstrous rail tracks.
But I heard the churp of a grasshopper.
And the beating of butterfly wings.

At home, in the depths of my wardrobe,
I cherish a bundle of clothes.
Hand-knitted cardigans,
a jumble of things,
that my son wore,
when he was small.

Gill Hartley

Rita Henshaw, who instigated and runs the Childless Parents' group within the Compassionate Friends, sent me this beautiful reading from the Book of Wisdom. I found it very comforting and have since passed it on to many other grieving parents. These words can apply equally to those who have lost a treasured daughter.

The Premature Death of a Virtuous Man.
The virtuous man, though he die before his time, will find rest.

Length of days is not what makes age honourable,
Nor the number of years the true measure of life;

Understanding, this is man's grey hairs,
Untarnished life, this is ripe old age.

He has sought to please God, so God has loved him;
As he was living among sinners he has been taken up.

He has been carried off so that evil may not warp his understanding
or treachery seduce his soul;

For the fascination of evil throws good things into the shade,
And the whirlwind of desire corrupts a simple heart.

Coming to perfection in so short a while, he achieved long life;

His soul being pleasing to the Lord,
He has taken him quickly from the wickedness around him.

Yet people look on, uncomprehending;
It does not enter their heads
That grace and mercy await the chosen of the Lord
And protection, his holy ones.

The Book of Wisdom Ch.4 v 7 – 15
The Jerusalem Bible

To everything there is a season, and a time to every purpose
under the heaven; A time to be born, and a time to die; a time to
plant, and a time to pluck that which is planted.

Ecclesiastes 3:1

We have suffered unimaginable pain and yet there are moments, as the following poem describes, when we feel comforted and very aware that there is so much we do not understand. I sometimes reflect that despite the pain of losing Will, I have never, ever wished that I had not had those precious years with him and would go through all this again rather than not have had him in my life.

154

Transformation

One summer's day, reclining on a cool
And willow-shaded bank beside a pool
I saw a creature leave the water there
And climbing up a reed stem, reach the air.
Drawn by instinct rather than by reason
Summoned by nature in its fitting season
To leave its world of water, mud and slime
And into air and sunshine slowly climb.
Then, as I watched this creature, I could see
Its body split apart. It seemed to me
That this was death - for every creature dies
But then, before my wide and startled eyes,
Emerging from this creature, shining, new,
Appeared a body clad in brilliant hue
Which spread limp wings to harden in the sun
Then flew away, its new life just begun.

I watched its jewel-like flight, its darting speed,
And then my gaze reverted to the reed.
This dragonfly, with colours gleaming bright
Whose iridescence shimmered in the light
Seemed unrelated to that tawdry thing
Whose husk, with lifeless feet, remained to cling
Upon the reed stem. Thus, I pondered death
And wondered when we draw our latest breath,
That we might die, and likewise be reborn
And into new existence may be drawn.
Dear Bobbie, still I see you lying there
I stooped to place a kiss upon your hair
But was it you who lay so still and white
Within the narrow coffin of my sight?
Or had you heard a call – not of this Earth
To summon you to glorious rebirth?
And are you now of wondrous form and state
That my poor mind can hardly contemplate?
So I believe, and hope that I shall find
Upon that day I leave my husk behind
That, like the dragonfly, whose wings unfurled

To free it from its dim and watery world,
So may my spirit on that final day
From time and space's confines, break away
And leave this earthly living in the past
To join you in the air of Heaven at last.

S J Collins, *TCF Parent*
Written following the death of
his youngest daughter, Deborah

I don't know who wrote the following poem but it is beautiful...

I thought that time would stop if you had died
That sun and moon and stars would disappear
The earth itself might vanish into darkness
If I had lost a life I held so dear
But though you're gone the sun still heralds the day
And darkness only brings a brief respite
The world goes on, and those who never knew you
Just cannot know the grief that's in my heart.

Yet even in that grief I keep the gladness
That comes from having loved you and been loved
And even in my anguish and my sorrow
Somehow your presence seems to ease my aching heart.
I see your smile and still share in your laughter
I talk to you and feel that you are near
I know that somehow you can still be with me
To help me bear the grief that's ever here.
I so believe that love can live forever
That happiness of memory conquers pain
And although the world seems empty now without you
I know that sometime we will meet again.

Writer unknown

Walk on the wild side...
When you died the world stopped turning,
the stars went out, one by one.
The moon man's face lost his smile
the sun forgot how to shine.

I walked by the tear filled river,
where willows wept with despair,
cormorants wore their mourning black
and the heron stood so still.

I longed for you at my side
with your familiar loping walk,
and listened for your voice in the silence
heard nothing but a gull's empty call.

I sank to my knees
on the moss-clad bank,
remembering the happy child.
who filled my days with laughter
and my heart with endless joy.

My darling, I try to be happy for you
as you spend your days with God,
but I am human and selfish
and grieve for all I have lost.

I'll endeavour to hold to God's promise
of a new world order to come,
when our tears are dried
and we dance on Heaven's streets,
reunited in our love.

Gill Hartley

One Saturday morning, 23 weeks after Will's death, I awoke knowing it was going to be one of "those days". The all too familiar pit in my stomach, the feeling of dread and despair was particularly strong. In one of the kitchen drawers I keep supplements, vitamin pills and such like. On this particular morning I opened this drawer and noticed a slip of paper I had never seen before. Written on the paper, in Will's familiar hand-writing, were the words, "Font of, water of, life without payment. Rev 21. 1-6." I knew, even before I picked up my bible, that the words were from Will's favourite bible passage from Revelation 21. This beautiful reading contains the wonderful promise, "He will wipe every tear from their eyes. There will be no more death or mourning or crying or pain, for the old order of things has passed away." Will was a great believer in a New Heaven and a New Earth and I knew this was a message from him, to help me through the day.

> *"¹ Then I saw a new heaven and a new earth, for the first heaven and the first earth had passed away, and there was no longer any sea. ²I saw the Holy City, the new Jerusalem, coming down out of heaven from God, prepared as a bride beautifully dressed for her husband. ³And I heard a loud voice from the throne saying, "Now the dwelling of God is with men, and he will live with them. They will be his people, and God himself will be with them and be their God. ⁴He will wipe every tear from their eyes. There will be no more death or mourning or crying or pain, for the old order of things has passed away."*
>
> *⁵He who was seated on the throne said, "I am making everything new!" Then he said, "Write this down, for these words are trustworthy and true."*
>
> *⁶He said to me: "It is done. I am the Alpha and the Omega, the Beginning and the End. To him who is thirsty I will give to drink without cost from the spring of the water of life. ⁷He who overcomes will inherit all this, and I will be his God and he will be my son.*

I rarely dream about Will, which is a disappointment to me. But one dream holds much hope for me and I will share it with you. I dreamed that Will had returned, but not as the young adult he was when he died, but as a young child. I was so thrilled to have him back and as I held him in my arms, I asked him, "Will, did you know you had died?" He looked at me and as his eyes met mine, I began to wake up. I began to weep, not wanting to re-enter my world of pain and my husband said I cried out, "No, no, it's true, it's true..." At that moment I felt someone leaning over me and a voice, clear and distinct said, "It's all right. I love you." I cannot explain that, it was not my husband, although he heard me cry out, he did not hear the voice I heard. The fact that the voice cut into my dream convinces me that it was God, possibly Will, but more likely to be God.

I like to believe that our children are still there for us, living in a different dimension but still with us. After Will died, one or two people said that perhaps in Will's time, his father and I are already with him. I find that a comforting thought, we cannot understand eternity, it is beyond our comprehension, but I do have to believe that there is something better to come for all of us. We live in a fallen world and because we do, these tragedies occur. But one day it will, as my son believed, all change and we will gaze upon the faces of our loved ones in delighted recognition. And what a day that will be.

Perhaps one day my grief will grow
Into hope:
Hope that I can use
All I have learnt
To make a difference to someone else.

Hope that I will no longer
Wear my pain
Like a badge on my sleeve,
Or let it consume me so totally
That it becomes the sum of who I am.
Hope that whether or not
I believe we will meet again
Still I can behave as if we will,
So that you can be proud of me.

Hope that in our own time
I will travel far enough
To be worthy to have known you.
Hope that I will know in my heart
That to let go the pain
Is to let in the love,
And give it room to grow.

Hope that one day my soul
Will be so full of love
That there will not be room for anything else.
Then joy, and not grief only,
Will be mine.

Kay Allen

Do not think that Death...

Do not think that death can take me from you,
for I loved you and I love you still.
God did not decree that love should have a span,
confined, with life, to three score years and ten.
Love endures for ever, else it is a sham.

Don't imagine guilt about the more you could have done,
or feel you failed because you let me down,
I probably was unaware of your supposed neglect,
And even if I noticed, or was hurt, you are forgiven:
Our love too precious to be thus soured for long.

So in those midnight hours of wakeful grief
don't cry! – talk to me.
And listen: for be assured I will be speaking words
of comfort as I did before.
I love you still, with love more strong than death.
I will be with you, never fear,
I am.
And I will never let you go.
Don't you give up on me!

Kip Bennet

Hope
Like me, the garden is desolate,
the mantle of winter has cast us both down.
Seed heads have replaced the flowers,
the rose arch is a bower of thorns.
The hammock where we swung on sunlit evenings,
stands dormant in the dank, anaemic air.
Everything looks so abandoned,
bleak and starved of light.
The garden, like me, is bereaved,
now summer has turned into night.

This morning, I searched the sleeping garden,
trod the sodden, yellowed grass,
knelt amongst the hibernating bushes,
cast aside the crumbling leaves,

and then I found
a thrusting shoot of crocus.

Gill Hartley
From 'My True Son' 2008

Whilst Will was in hospital in Leicester, he asked the nurses to buy a Christmas card for him to give to Edwin and me. We will always treasure it, the writing is like a child's, as Will could only write on the pad, held by the nurse. Underneath the message from him, he wrote "Footprints". He also received some little cards from friends from church, with the Footprints poem and he asked me to put the cards on the window in front of him, where he could see them. There is always some debate as to the true writer of this much loved poem but, whoever actually wrote these words, they hold a lot of significance to me and brought comfort to Will – and that makes them very special.

Footprints

One night I dreamed I was walking
Along the beach with the Lord.
Many scenes from my life flashed across the sky.
In each scene I noticed footprints in the sand.
Sometimes there were two sets of footprints.
Other times there were one set of footprints.
This bothered me because I noticed that
During the low periods of my life when I was
Suffering from anguish, sorrow, or defeat,
I could see only one set of footprints,
So I said to the Lord, "You promised me,
Lord, that if I followed You,
You would walk with me always.
But I noticed that during the most trying periods
Of my life there have only been
One set of prints in the sand.
Why, When I have needed You most,
You have not been there for me?"
The Lord replied,
"The times when you have seen only one set of footprints
Is when I carried you."

Mary Stevenson

It was Will's last message to us…

Helplines

The Compassionate Friends (TCF)
Help and support for bereaved parents and their families.
TCF National Office: 53 North Street, Bristol BS3 1EN
Tel: 0845 1203785   Helpline: 0845 1232304
Email: info@tcf.org.uk
www.tcf.org.uk

The Child Bereavement Charity
Supporting families and educating professionals when a child dies
and when a child is bereaved.
The Saunderton Estate, Wycombe Road, Saunderton
Buckinghamshire HP14 4BF
Tel: 01494 568900
Email: enquiries@childbereavement.org.uk

Care for the Family
(Bereaved Parents' Network)
A national charity which aims to promote strong family life and to
help those who face family difficulties.
Tel: 029 2081 0800
Email:mail@cff.org.uk
www.careforthefamily.org.uk

The Child Death Helpline
www.childdeathhelpline.org.uk
A Freephone service for anyone affected by the death of a child.
Tel: 0800 282 986
Freephone number for ALL mobile phones: 0808 800 6019

Author's profits and royalties from the sale of this book
are donated to "The Compassionate Friends"

MOORLEYS
Print & Publishing

As a well established publisher we add several new titles to our list each year.
We also undertake private publications and commissioned works.

Our range includes

Books of Verse
Devotional Poetry
Recitations for Children
Humorous Monologues

Drama
Bible Plays
Sketches
Christmas, Passiontide,
Easter & Harvest Plays
Demonstrations

Resource Books
Assembly Material
Easy Use Music Books for Piano and Keyboard
Children's Addresses
Prayers
Worship & Preaching
Books for Speakers

Activity Books
Quizzes & Puzzles

Church Stationery
Notice Books & Cradle Roll Certificates

Associated Lists and Imprints
Cliff College Publishing
Nimbus Press
MET (Headway)
Social Work Christian Fellowship

For up to date news, special offers & information on our full list of titles, please visit our website at www.moorleys.co.uk

Alternatively send a stamped addressed C5 envelope for our current catalogue, or consult your local Christian Bookshop, who will either stock or be able to obtain our titles.